ISBN 0 901367 30 3

Merseyside at War

A Day-by-Day Diary of the 1940-1941 Bombing

by Rodney Whitworth

Scouse Press: Liverpool L8 3SB 051-727 2727

Worshippers in their Sunday-best enter a relatively undamaged part of the Parish Church of St Nicholas, on the Liverpool Pier Head, for a service.

To the Memory of the many children

killed or maimed during the Liverpool Blitz

and especially

to a schoolboy, John Seafield, aged 12 years,

killed by a Parachute Mine

on the night of 10th November, 1940

During the Blitz, Rodney Whitworth, son of a Liverpool policeman, was a schoolboy, Liverpool Cathedral chorister, and A.R.P. Messenger. At the end of the War he was serving with a Mine Disposal Unit in Northern Ireland.

For a number of years he worked in Bahrain, Kuwait and Kenya, until becoming a probation officer in Manchester in 1962.

Since 1974 he has been Head of Penal Social Work in the Tayside Region. He married a Liverpool girl, and has three sons.

INTRODUCTION

As the years go by it becomes ever more important that the personal memories of Merseysiders on the civilian battlefront of the Second World War should be preserved. Those who lived through the blitz, who came under fire from enemy bombers, can hardly forget the experience; but others, who are too young to remember or were not yet born, should also learn about those momentous days.

Everyone who was in the Merseyside area during the blitz had a personal story to tell, usually one of miraculous escapes, often of tragedy - and always full of tales of comradeship, of working together and, of course, stories that reflected the irrepressible, in-bred Scouse humour.

Rodney Whitworth's *Merseyside at War* is a day-by-day diary of the 1940-1941 bombing. It will vividly bring back those days to the Merseysiders lucky enough to have lived through them. As Winston Churchill said, "This was their finest Hour". The book complements and amplifies - but by no means supplants - the companion-volume *Bombers over Merseyside* which was first published in 1943 and reprinted in facsimile by Scouse Press in 1983. For *Bombers over Merseyside* was a war-time effort, intended to boost morale and keep spirits up during the darkest days this country ever had to suffer. That story is therefore necessarily incomplete, for much of what really happened was necessarily concealed, or had to be carefully couched in terms that would not reveal useful information to the enemy.

The architectural gaps and scars left by Hitler's bombs may long have healed or been repaired (or replaced with a post-war building blight), both in Liverpool and on the Wirral; but there is much else that will never be the same again. Even the old wartime expressions have been put to a more peacable use. The word "fighter" is more likely to refer to a boxer than a Spitfire; and a "blockbuster", formerly one of the most feared high-explosive bombs (like the dreaded parachute mines described in this book), now denotes a large, heavy and trashy novel. (I once had an idea for one but it was - "shot down in flames"...) People who stumbled home in the blackout - total darkness without street-lamps or even car lights, almost unimaginable to the town-dweller - now speak of temporary moments of forgetfulness as "blackouts". Even the word "blitz" itself (a derisive abbreviation of Hitler's threatened "lightning war", or *Blitzkrieg*), is now defined in the dictionary as nothing more terrible than "a period of great activity for some special purpose"!

We have, alas, also lost for ever that wonderful wartime spirit of friendship and camaraderie which brought people so close together during the blitz. Everyone, from all walks of life, had the common aim of defeating a common enemy. Total strangers suddenly became firm friends, swapping bomb stories, sharing rations, or helping each other out to replace household goods buried under tons of rubble. It was almost as if Hitler had suddenly and unwittingly introduced everyone to everyone else, and at a stroke removed the traditional reserve of the Englishman. No doubt there were isolated incidents of robbery or of looting in the blackout after the bombing. But if there were, I have yet to hear of any; nor of a single instance of an old person being "mugged" (a word which still had only a kindly Scouse meaning in those days). Yet poverty during the 1930s, before the welfare state, was acute in Liverpool, and of a degree unimaginable by even the neediest welfare state claimant of today. The English - no, British - spirit of fair play extended even to the enemy. On numerous occasions German airmen who parachuted to earth were given cups of tea by the very householders they had just tried to kill. "Well, what else could I do?" was the usual explanation.

There was a determination to work together, to weather every crisis, a spirit of "Business as Usual" that would be impossible to match today. For example, during the 1941 May blitz the premises of the Liverpool Daily Post and Echo were severely damaged (see *Bombers over Merseyside*, mentioned above). There was no water, gas or electricity, all telephone lines were cut, and machinery was severely damaged. But, against all the odds, the next day's issue appeared as usual. No-one demanded danger money, "dirty" money (for working in mud left by firefighters) or overtime payment - let alone engaging in the inter-union "who-does-what" demarcation squabbles that later played their part in speeding Merseyside's industrial, shipping and dockland decline.

It is sad to report that Rodney Whitworth, the talented author of Merseyside at War, died during its preparation for print, although he was able to inspect it during its proof stage. We are grateful to his widow, Mrs Joan Whitworth, for her help in seeing it through the press. He himself dedicated this little book to the memory of a schoolboy who was killed by a parachute mine in 1940. We hope that this book will serve also as a memorial to Mr Whitworth.

Many of the wartime photographs are here published for the first time, for most official pictures by the war photographers of the time showing the devastation were then for obvious reasons censored. Many have only comparatively recently become public property. Acknowledgement is made to the many anonymous photographers, who often worked under dangerous condition; also to the *Radio Times Hulton Picture Library*. Val Taylor was responsible for the typesetting, and Michael Scott designed the book. And the work of *Printfine Ltd.*, who produced it, amply demonstrates that fine printing still flourishes on Merseyside.

Fritz Spiegl

Liverpool 1940-1941

Foreword

June 1940 was for the German U-Boats the most successful month of the war so far, with sixty three ships totalling 355,431 tons sent to the bottom of the sea. The total of Allied shipping losses for that month was nearly 600,000 tons, a figure far in excess of the capacity of the British shipyards to make good. It was no wonder that Winston Churchill was later to comment, "The only thing that ever really frightened me during the war was the U-Boat peril . . . I was even more anxious about this battle than I had been about the glorious air fight called the Battle of Britain."

After Dunkirk the Royal Navy was ill-equipped to meet the U-Boat offensive, convoys from North America were often unescorted until they were within three days of the North Channel. Only the failure of the German High Command to sustain the U-Boat offensive saved the nation from starvation and ultimate defeat. The U-Boat building programme had not yet been given high enough priority to establish an underseas fleet capable of mounting and sustaining a large scale continuous offensive. Without the support of Luftwaffe attacks upon British port installations there was little chance that the U-Boat arm alone could bring the war to a speedy conclusion.

In July 1940 Grand Admiral Raeder, Commander in Chief of the German Navy, implored Hitler to authorise a concentrated air attack upon Liverpool. He felt that destruction of this vital port would bring Britain to its knees, and advised Hitler that after the destruction of Liverpool the British people would listen to a peace offer without Germany having to resort to an invasion of the British islands. Raeder's advice went unheeded; and it was not until August 1940 that air attacks of any real significance were made against the city and port of Liverpool. It was then too late. The British people had weathered the storm; Dunkirk and the shipping losses in the Atlantic were behind them. As for the people of Liverpool, they, together with the rest of the nation, were living up to the spirit of the Foreign Minister's reply to Hitler's offer of peace: Britain, he said, was ruled by a spirit of inexorable resolve. She would not give up the fight.

Mr. Whitworth's excellent collection of facts and anecdotes illustrates very clearly the total failure of the German High Command to gauge or understand the utter determination of the British people to resist aggression and to defend their country. Neither the U-Boats or the Luftwaffe could overcome this resolve unless their combined efforts were totally co-ordinated and concentrated upon strangulation of Britain's sea lines of communications. This never occurred. Hitler thought that he could terrorise the British people into submission by random attacks upon our cities. He was wrong. The story of Liverpool 1940-1941 is now part of our heritage. No military victory was ever more heroic or important than the victory of the people of our cities.

Rear Admiral E.N. Poland, C.B., C.B.E.,
Director of Undersea Warfare 1962-1965

DANGER

SMALL ANTI-PERSONNEL BOMB

BEWARE OF THESE BOMBS WHICH ARE VERY DESTRUCTIVE AND ARE MEANT TO DO YOU HARM.

THEY MAY BE FOUND

– LIKE THIS – OR – LIKE THIS –

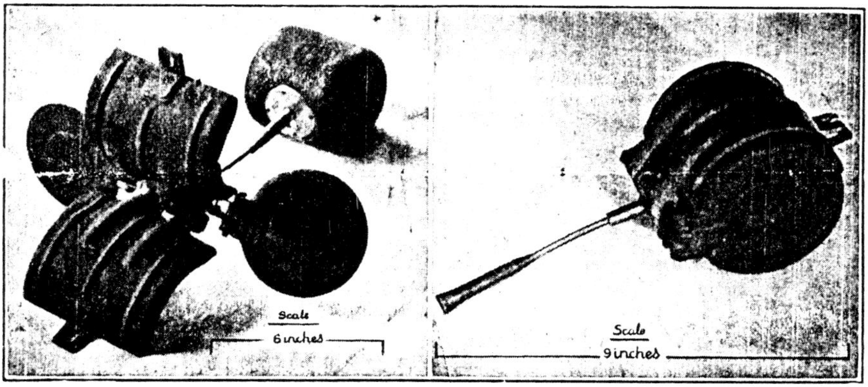

BOMB WITH CASING OPEN | BOMB WITH CASING CLOSED

IF YOU SEE THEM DO NOT TOUCH, KEEP AWAY AND REPORT THEM TO THE WARDENS OR POLICE

DO NOT TOUCH SUSPICIOUS OBJECTS REPORT THEM TO WARDENS OR POLICE

Issued by the Ministry of Home Security

20,000 10/41 (16411) 38956/803 30,000 12/41 K.H.K Gp. 8.

Report by Chief Constable of Liverpool

The following abstract was taken from a report made by the Chief Constable of Liverpool to the Watch Committee:

"For seven consecutive nights from 1st May to 8th May, raids of varying intensity were made on Liverpool. Although most of the damage was to public buildings, churches and commercial industrial premises, the extent of the raids can be judged from the total destruction of 4,400 houses, serious damage to 16,400 and slight damage to a further 45,000. Water mains were affected to such an extent that over 700 repairs were required, many involving up to 50 yards of main. There were some 80 cases of damage to sewers.

235 unexploded bombs were reported in the city and there were some 500 roads in the city closed to the traffic, most of these roads being in the central area and in many cases re-opening was long delayed owing to the necessity of the large-scale demolition work.

Owing to the shortage of water, a great deal of relay pumping had to be done by the Fire Brigade causing more traffic difficulties and the laying of several lines of 6 inch steel piping proved a serious obstacle to traffic until proper ramps had been constructed. In addition, the Air Ministry required the movement of 79 aircraft right through the centre of the city for urgent shipment at the North Docks.

The worst night was that of the 3rd/4th of May during which there were over 600 incidents representing a large fire area. On this night, the central area of the city had its three telephone exchanges destroyed by fire and for many hours no electric current was available. Practically every tramcar route was seriously affected and on the 4th of May only 13.% of the total route mileage was in operation. During the night some 400 fires were attended by the Fire Brigade and many more were dealt with in other ways.

The total number of Air Raids 'Red Alert' received in Liverpool was 509. During the raids a total of 2,596 persons were killed, 2,548 were seriously injured, of whom 154 subsequently died, and 1,600 were slightly injured.

(Sgd.) H. Winstanley
Chief Constable
1941"

Bombs and Mines

The disposal of unexploded bombs was generally the duty of the Bomb Disposal Units of the Royal Engineers. Parachute mines and other types of mines were dealt with and disposed of by the Royal Navy assisted by the Bomb Disposal companies of the Royal Engineers.

According to the War Office Statistics, the daily average of unexploded bombs dropped on Great Britain (excluding bombs dropped on Royal Naval and Royal Air Force establishments) for the period 21st September 1940 to 5th July 1941 was eighty-four. Of these, an average of 8.5 per cent exploded some time after they fell. The majority of these were probably time bombs and the balance may have exploded owing to the shock caused by the explosions of other bombs which fell near them. The remaining 91.5 per cent of unexploded bombs were 'duds' and included a proportion of about 6.5 per cent of time bombs. (German time bombs were set to explode at any time between 0 and 80 hours after they fell).

Further statistics showed that of the unexploded bombs disposed of in the period October 1940 to May 1941, approximately 66 per cent were 50 kg; 27 per cent were 250 kg; 4 per cent were 500 kg, and 3 per cent were 1000 kg or over.

The most common sizes of high-explosive bombs were the 50 and 250 kg types, but 500, 1,000 and bigger sizes up to 1,800 kg were encountered. They held about half their weight of explosive and were fitted with one or sometimes two fuses; some were fitted with fuses that would explode if they were removed. Others contained a clock mechanism which could be set to function between 0 and 80 hours after falling.

Time bombs were usually the 250 kg or 500 kg type, though cases are known where 50 kg and 1,000 kg types were fitted with time fuses.

Other bombs of the incendiary and anti-personnel types:-

German Incendiary Bombs

Three types of incendiary bombs were dropped on Liverpool during the war—the small 1 kg; the 250 kg; and the 500 kg. The small 1 kg type (Plate 5), had a hollow, cylindrical magnesium body filled with thermite, and a tail usually painted green.

Some of these bombs had a small bursting-charge contained in a steel tube screwed into the back of the bomb, and hidden under the tail unit. This burster-charge exploded after the bomb had been alight from one to two minutes.

The 250 kg Incendiary Bomb (usually referred to as an 'Oil Bomb')

It looked like a 250 kg high explosive bomb. It was filled with oil and had a bursting-charge of about 2½ lbs. of high explosive.

The C300 (flam) Incendiary Bomb

This looked like the 500 high explosive bomb; it was a sensitive missile containing high-explosive and could be removed only by R.E. Units specially trained in its disposal.

Anti-Personnel Bombs

There were two types of German anti-personnel bombs: they were the 2 kg and the S.C.10, which weighed 12 kg.

The 2 kg anti-personnel bomb is shown in Plate IV. Unexploded bombs of this type were highly sensitive. They could cause death, or fatal injury, up to 25 yards, and wounds up to 150 yards, but caused little damage to property.

The bombs were painted bright yellow with a red stripe on the braking wings. They were also coloured Field Grey with a $\frac{3}{4}$" wide yellow stripe on the body and on the inside and outside of the wings.

The 12 kg anti-personnel bomb is shown in Plate VII. It was about $3\frac{3}{4}$" in diameter and $22\frac{1}{2}$" long, including the tail. It contained 1—2 lbs. of high-explosive only, being designed primarily for splinter effect; it was fitted with a mechanical fuse which was designed to explode the bomb, on, or very shortly after, impact.

Parachute Mines (familiarly known as Land Mines) (Plate VII)

Parachute mines varied in shape and size. They were roughly cylindrical and up to 12 ft. long and 2'2" in diameter; rounded at the front end with an attachment for a parachute at the back.

They were made of aluminium, often painted grey. The parachutes were approximately 15 feet in diameter when opened, and were usually made of green silk.

These mines were liable to detonate either magnetically or acoustically, or through ground vibration. The Royal Navy was responsible for the rendering unexploded mines 'safe' as far as possible, after which Bomb Disposal Units of the R.E.'s were responsible for their removal and subsequent disposal.

'G' Mine (Plate VII)

These mines were dropped like bombs, without parachutes, and looked like bombs. They were painted light blue and were fitted with tail fins of bakelized cardboard, coloured light brown on the surface, and about $\frac{1}{8}$" thick, which broke off on impact.

Their disposal was the duty of the Royal Navy, assisted by Bomb Disposal Squads of the R.E.'s.

Anti-Aircraft Shells

Anti-aircraft shells were of two types:-

1. Those of 4·5″ — 3″ diameter
2. Those of 1·6″ diameter which were highly sensitive and unsafe to handle.

Craters

The size of craters found when a buried bomb exploded varied with the depth of penetration and the nature of the soil. The average figures were:-

For a 50 kg bomb : 10-15 ft. diameter
For a 250 kg bomb : 18-25 ft. diameter
For a 500 kg bomb : 25-30 ft. diameter
For parachute mines : 50 -80 ft. diameter

St Michael's Church, Pitt Street, Liverpool, which was damaged during the night raid of May 5/6th 1941.

Rescuers searching the rubble of the Custom House pub, wrecked on Friday, 11th October 1940.

has bred up only one completely new craft. It is a sign of the meaning of total war that this should be the craft of burrowing for broken bodies among the ruin of homes. There has never before been the opportunity to develop an intense scientific interest n the behaviour of broken buildings and the way their fragments lie. Until our own generation, it was hardly a matter of general concern that a house could collapse in three different ways—by total disintegration into mixed rubble, by the curving fall of roofs and floors, held at one side while the other swung downwards, or by the breaking of floors in the middle while their sides held, so that they formed a 'V' beneath the arms of which men on the storey below might be preserved alive.

The Rescue Man was the new technician of the blitz. His pre-war training taught him much, but when the bombs fell he learned much more. He learned how to tunnel through shifting masses of rubble on unstable footings, using whatever head-support he could find—sometimes his prepared lengths of timber, but sometimes a kitchen table or a wardrobe-frame which he pushed before him as he went on. He learned to be very delicate with his big hands, for if he could not withdraw a lump of brick-and-mortar without disturbing, by a hair's breadth, the broken timber beside it he might bring the tons of stuff above down upon him.

He learned the strange ways of furniture—how a piano might fall half forward and lock with a chair, far below the surface of a dense mass of debris, leaving beneath its tilted keyboard just one clear space with a woman pinned in it. He grew used to clearing a passage for himself among materials under tremendous pressures and learned to take advantage of their stresses so that when he had finished his picking and hollowing, the sides and roof of his zig-zag corridor were firmly held, and he could come back by the way he had gone in.

His was the most laborious of all the tasks of civil defence. He had been known to keep straining away at a difficult piece of rescue for seventeen hours on end. His work had also its special risks. Underground his fate was always poised precariously over his head. Above ground he often worked under a tottering wall and lacked the time to deal with it. What couldn't be shored must be ignored. In basements there might be water from broken pipes, rising steadily towards the roof as the parties struggled to get in and release someone, or to get out with him. Gas often leaked from fractured mains or household pipes; it might make any enclosed space into an immediate fatal trap. And so often there was fire, to give the rescuers minutes instead of hours, and threaten them as they hurried.

But there was another side to this. Rescue was not only a craft, it was a calling; it took firm hold on the tough builders' labourers and the others who practiced it and filled them with pride and interest in their work. For they had a quarry. They were working towards a living being—or several. The warden, or the woman next door, had told them definitely of people under that wreckage who might well be alive. So every now and again as they struggled noisily forward the party leader would call for silence and they would strain their ears for voices, a muffled cry, even the noise of breathing. As they drew nearer they might be able to talk to their 'patient', perhaps for the hours that it took to get through those last few impenetrable feet. Later still they could give the kid, or the old girl, or grandpa, a drink—water or stimulant out of their cupped hand.

This was what gripped you, what made worthwhile the hours of heavy labour in the thundering blackness—this prospect of 'getting the old boy out'. It was something you liked to do yourself, and your party, and when you'd get to him you had been known to pick him up, cold-shoulder the stretcher party with a muttered "this one's mine", and take him to the ambulance in your own arms. Though the ones you rescued never knew who you were, and couldn't very often find you to thank you afterwards, you could (and did) find out from the Town Hall or the Hospital how they were getting on. The satisfaction was therefore greater if you were working in your own area for your own people. "We done all the rough work, see, twelve hours it might 'a bin, and then they want to send us home and let those reinforcement chaps from ..... get the old boy out!"

Not if you could help it!

First Aid Party

The First Aid Party, waiting in its depot, was ordered out by the Control Centre to any spot where bombs had caused injury. Four men and a driver made a party. Each was an experienced first aid worker. Perhaps before the war he was a member of the Red Cross, St. John or St. Andrew's Society; he was in any case a man drawn temperamentally to the work of healing, ready to face the full risk of war but happiest in one of its most constructive callings. His work did not call for the highest medical skill, but for speed, sound judgement and steady nerve.

The Party's first task was to help the Rescue Men to release trapped casualties. Then they must decide whom to treat, whom to send home; of the more serious cases, who should go to hospital and who to the First Aid Post. On the soundness of these rough and ready diagnoses lives would depend. It was dark: bombs were falling: perhaps it was raining: and there was not a second to be lost. In the earlier days of the attack, before the practice grew up of sending an 'Incident Doctor' to the scene, the First Aid Parties made these crucial decisions unaided as they bandaged and splinted in the night. And the doctors at hospital or at the Post usually found they had decided rightly.

The Ambulance Driver

They went out together, driver and attendant, from their depot to the bombed site; and it was the driver's business to get there, whatever craters, fires, trailing wires, boulders or hoses might be in her path. She had volunteered because she had been used to driving her own car, most likely, or the family's. "Civil Occupation: Housewife", she had written on the application form: or "Typist", or occasionally, "None"—what they called a Bright Young Thing.

She had shuddered at a dead bird on the footpath, and now she was going to deal with death and mutilation in forms as horrible as any battlefield had ever seen. If she told the truth she might confess that when she swung her ambulance out of the depot gates that first night, what set her heart thumping was not the bombs but the thought of facing and dealing with her first casualties.

Yet when she got there she could think only of the people she had come to help. Before very long nothing could move her. To be sure, it was unnerving when you found that, by some mistake, what you had been given as a casualty was in fact a corpse. It was worse still, for a second, when a 'corpse' suddenly asked for a drink of water. That worried you. But having to drive for miles under bombs or through flames, or to sit for hours in a blitz waiting for your casualties, to all outward appearance did not.

First Aid Post

There were the doctor, the trained nurse and the nursing auxiliaries. They had an area with something like 15,000 people in it for their own. They took what the ambulances brought them. They worked away as though there were no air raids, and no such thing had ever happened as a bomb falling on a post like theirs, adding the names of its staff to their own casualty lists.

This was the 'fixed' post. There were also mobile posts or units, made up in the same way, on call to any 'Incident Doctor', or ready to reinforce a hard-pressed fixed post or even a hospital. At a bomb incident, it might fall to one of the nursing auxiliaries to follow a rescue worker down a tunnel into a basement where people were trapped, and there to give them what help was possible. She might sit there for hours relieving their pain and giving them the comfort of her presence until rescue was complete.

The splendid work of the Emergency Hospitals and their staffs is not touched upon in these pages.

The Women's Voluntary Services

Sometimes they wore uniform, sometimes overalls. Sometimes just a green armlet over 'kitchen dress'. On the shoulders of these million women whose home duties forbade their doing whole-time war work fell much of the burden of the after-raid welfare services. Without them the job could never have been done.

On the morning of Saturday, 10th M
1941 the sunlight streams through
the burnt-out roof of St Luke's,
at the top of Bold Street. The chu
is now a memorial to the Merseys
blitz, preserved in its damaged sta
with gardens offering rest and
reflection to Liverpool office worke

Mossley Hill Church.

Two small survivors have rescued their teddy-bear.

They knew that too much organising wasn't a good thing, and that people would sort themselves out very well if left alone at the right moment. They filled hours with washing-up and washing towels, serving breakfasts and dishing out uncountable tea cups, slipping home—if they could—to see to their own husbands' dinners and then back to reach down the plates for their charges.

But Rest Centres were only a part. They staffed the brightly coloured Queens' Messenger Convoys that went into the raided towns and cooked and served hot food in the first hours of muddle and distress. They drove and worked the mobile canteens, cutting, stewing and tea brewing; sometimes on the morning after, but often in the blitz when the civil defence workers as well as the homeless needed quick sustenance.

They drove vans day and night, sometimes taking people to shelters or centres from homes at which the flames were already licking, sometimes just moving blankets. Later in the blitz their 'housewives' service' organised the hundred and one small errands of compassion that are so large a part of work after the raid.

'After the raid' was an elastic term. W.V.S. women might have to get up at four in the morning for days on end to come from their own peaceful town as reinforcing parties and be at their Centre before the All Clear. Or they might be seen walking in the blitz from their home to the Rest Centre nearby, aproned and with basins and colanders held above their heads against falling shrapnel. Mobile canteens often came in with radiators, windscreens and drivers' cabins pitted with holes from machine gun bullets and bomb fragments. In the port, as the women fed tea and sandwiches to dockers working an urgent load in the dark, a nearby bomb blew them and their canteen into the dock basin—icy water on their backs and scalding hot tea down their fronts at the same instant.

Like all other civil defenders they had their own homes bombed, and their own relatives killed, as they worked.

Two Telephonists

(i) *Control Centre*

She took messages from the wardens and passed them to the service chiefs nearby; or she passed their instructions to the depots where the service parties waited. It was a simple job. All it needed was a clear head, a total disregard for bombs, and the kind of self-control that could take a message about a big incident somewhere in one's own street and pass it on as though nothing had happened.

Often bombs fell near enough to make the floor of the Control Room heave; sometimes nearer, so as to bounce the rows of girls a foot out of their chairs and back again; or nearer still, to put the lights out and leave everything in darkness till the emergency lighting came on. Or you might get a direct hit. Control Centres had done more than once.

(ii) G.P.O. *Exchange*

"Number please? Would you mind speaking up—there's some noise going on round here." In heavy raids, the girl operators dealing with emergency calls at the G.P.O exchanges were workmanlike about their duties. Sometimes they could sit at their switchboards in shelter, but if anything went wrong they or their men colleagues might have to climb to a top floor and there handle special business while the raid went on. Bombs blasted in the windows of exchanges, incendiaries fired their buildings, ceilings and rooms filled with rubble, dust and smoke. Operators crouched beneath their switchboards to avoid flying bomb fragments and then got out to carry on.

The exchange might be a one-woman affair in a small village, on which depended the prospect of help for the civil defence services under one of those senseless and devastating attacks that did afflict villages. Then some elderly woman would sit at work for hours among the bombs and fires, all night and well into the next day. Upon her, as upon telephonists in every raided area, pivoted all the complex working of the defence machine.

The Messenger

Two extracts from official reports will tell the Messenger's story: This is the first:

> 'John Smith. Aged 16. Cyclist despatch rider (part-time). Normal civilian occupation: schoolboy.
>
> 'During last Thursday's enemy air attack, telephone communications were put out of action at an early hour. Smith maintained contact between the Report Centre and services in action by carrying operational messages on his bicycle, riding the whole time except for three short intervals, once when he dismounted to extinguish an incendiary bomb that had fallen in dangerous proximity to a wooden fence, and twice when he was forced to disentangle his cycle from loose telephone wires fallen across the roadway. The roads were also seriously obstructed by homb craters and debris, as high explosives were falling continuously in the district. Though exhausted from his efforts, he insisted on continuing to carry messages throughout the area all night. During the ten hours he was on duty, Smith was the main channel of communications with the services.'

This is the second:

> 'Particular praise is given by wardens to several boys who frankly confessed themselves frightened, but still did not hesitate to go

out on long and hazardous journeys, not even when flat tyres could have been used as an excuse. Among the messengers was a small pale boy who begged to be allowed to take a message, but the Chief Warden, feeling that the danger was too great for him, put him off time after time with various excuses, the final one being that he had no bicycle. "Please, sir", said the lad eagerly, "Billy will lend me his bicycle."

'After some hesitation the Chief Warden finally sent him off. After a long time he returned, breathless, wild-eyed and bleeding, and covered with dirt. He asked to speak to the Chief Warden privately. "Glad to see you back, my boy," said the Chief Warden as he bent down to listen to the lad's agitated whisper. "I daren't tell Billy, sir, but I've lost his bloody bicycle. I was blown off it, and when I got up I could only find the front wheel.'

The Policeman

There was nothing in civil defence that the policeman did not do. He reported incidents to the Control Centre, and got the services into action, as did the warden. He moved people from threatened shelters. If an unexploded bomb fell he warned the nearby householders, evacuated them, and diverted the traffic. When he came upon people trapped, he went to work to rescue them, until the specialist parties arrived. If they were injured, he applied a tourniquet or splint, or dressed their wounds.

Everywhere outside London it was his duty to take charge of an incident, co-ordinate the work of the parties, and give general direction to their operations. (In London this was the warden's responsibility). If incendiary bombs fell, he must help to put them out and to deal with the fires they caused, unless these were big enough to need the attendance of the fire brigade. He had been known to conduct fire-fighting himself; if all the pump crews were out, he could borrow appliances, muster wardens or civilians from the neighbourhood, connect up to the hydrants and get to work until the brigades attended. Was a shop front smashed and valuable goods exposed? It was the policeman who found members of the Home Guard and posted them as sentries or mounted guard himself if there was nothing more urgent to be done.

His continually varying work called always for personal initiative. All of it was responsible and all of it was dangerous. It meant activity in the open, under bombing, for as long as there was work to be done in his neighbourhood. Some of the rescue work done by the police takes rank with the most heroic episodes of that hazardous craft; in a heavy raid, when the calls on the rescue services were many, police constables might work for hours among the debris in imminent danger of death. When the raid was over, and the count of dead and injured had to be made, it fell to the police to keep the tally, to notify the next of kin, and to deal with the mass of enquiries from relatives and friends that descended upon them by every possible channel. They had to make known their tidings, often bitter and grievous, to people overwrought by their own personal experiences. There must be no failure in tact and kindness—and there was none.

Every one of these tasks grew directly out of the normal function of the police as upholders of order and guardians of the public welfare. One would hardly compare closely a street collision with the fall of a large bomb; yet both logically and in practice there are points of resemblance between them. So there came to be a saying among the police that an incident was just a large accident. The risks were more severe but the police were chosen and trained to face risk. The complexities were greater, but one learned to cope with them. The conditions of work were infinitely more difficult, but the issues at stake were greater and with experience one rose to the occasion.

All these extra burdens, and others not directly arising from civil defence, needed extra shoulders to carry them. So the Auxiliary Police War Rescue was recruited before the war and called into being on the outbreak. It was a whole-time force. The part-time Special Constables also played an essential part. It was a testimonial to all concerned—to the comradely spirit of the regulars, and the keen intelligence of the newcomers—that the latter so soon learned to show themselves in practice worthy of the traditions of the British police.

The police stood a little apart from civil defence, with their own functions of traffic control, movement of the public and preservation of order. But the distinction was more complete in theory than in practice. On the ground, the constable many a time worked shoulder to shoulder with the warden, the rescue men or the first aid party, just as he did outside the capital.

Defences of the City

The defence of Liverpool and the rest of Merseyside rested on the Fourth Anti-Aircraft Division commanded by Major General C.A.E. Cadell, whose Headquarters were at Chester. In addition to Liverpool the Division had to protect Barrow, Birmingham, Crewe, Coventry, Manchester and Ringway Airport but, in spite of the area's importance, increasing enemy air activity over Southern England forced anti-aircraft command to deploy a number of heavy guns to the south. On the 11th September, 1940, fifty-eight anti-aircraft guns were strategically positioned around the perimeter of the City but this number, according to the War Office (at least in theory) was sufficient for the sixteen-gun density aimed at by General Pile, which meant that, within a particular defence area, aircraft could be effectively engaged by a minimum of sixteen guns.

Anti-aircraft guns, in the main, were of three types. The 4.5 inch, the gun which hurled a high explosive shell weighing nearly half a hundredweight to a height of 8 miles in fifty seconds and the 3.7 inch which had almost as high a ceiling and a faster rate of fire but a smaller shell.

There were also some 3 inch guns which fired high explosive and shrapnel shells every three seconds. The lighter anti-aircraft guns were the Bofors and the Lewis machine gun. The Bofors weighed two tons and fired anything to 120 two-pound shells a minute to a height of 6,000 feet; the shells burst on impact.

The First World War Lewis gun was surprisingly successful, mounted singly, or in twin or quadruple for greater firing power. Its function was to hold off aircraft from low-level attacks.

In the closing months of 1940, 'Z' Batteries were placed at New Brighton and Sefton Park. They consisted of 20 large rocket projectors, capable of firing 4,000 rockets simultaneously.

To assist the gunners, Searchlight Detachments were dotted around the City of Liverpool. Each light was capable of producing 210,000,000 candlepower to probe the night sky with its beam.

The Searchlight Detachments were drafted to the Liverpool area from as far away as Orkney. A Corporal tells this story of the night of May 1st 1941:

> "The first night was not so bad, but the sirens sounded as the clock on the Liver Buildings said ten. The raid lasted six hours; but the real ordeal began on the next night. Incendiaries which rained down set fire to piles of timber lying about. The only sandbags available were on the Projector-pit. The bags came down a lot faster than they had been built.
>
> The following night, more than 100 incendiaries fell on the site, setting fire to the living hut and the cookhouse. The cook, who was

preparing a drop of soup, only knew that two of them came through the roof, and one dropped slap into the dixie of soup! Unfortunately, six of the incendiaries fell inside the Projector-pit one struck the number 4, putting him into hospital for a month.

Those fires had to be put out and all the men were brought almost to a state of collapse by the heat. The site was a shambles."

The crew endured this for a further three nights, until two high explosive bombs fell on the site, one almost on the generator and the other making a mess of the badly battered sleeping quarters. They had to wait nearly six months for their revenge, but on the night of November 1st 1941, a Junkers 88 flew over them at 200 feet. He stopped the best part of 86 rounds from their Lewis gun, for which they were given a category III (damaged) 'Bird'.

The balloon barrage will be remembered by many as they swung lazily backwards and forwards in the evening skies, the sunset glittering like gold on their silver skins and the puffs of smoke followed by flames, as they fluttered to earth when struck by lightning.

The usual type of barrage balloon used was a streamlined bag of rubber-proofed cotton fabric, specially treated, with a gas capacity of 19,150 cubic feet. Its length overall was about 63 ft. and its height just over 31 ft. The weight was approximately 550 lbs. and it was flown on a flexible steel cable.

The balloons were operated at medium heights thus preventing accurate aiming and dive-bombing, and at the same time leaving the upper air free for fighter-interception.

Finally, a word must be mentioned about the crews who operated the mobile smoke-screens (strange, long trucks with a large funnel placed at one end, billowing jet-black smoke into the evening sky) whose lot it was to camp under canvas in the Sefton Park area.

The Bombers over Liverpool

During 1940-41 the major types of aircraft used by the Luftwaffe *Kampfgeschwadern* (Fighting Squadrons) against Liverpool were:

Heinkel He 111

The Heinkel 111 low-wing monoplane was produced in nine variants and was powered by either two Junkers Jumo 211D-2 or Daimler Benz DB601A-1 engines. They proved too slow and were too lightly armed. The crew of five were housed together in the forward section of the aircraft, the philosophy behind this being to increase morale level; and this was certainly needed as the large glazed nose gave the pilot and the observer a very good view but made the whole crew extremely vulnerable. The maximum speed with a normal bomb-load was 255 m.p.h. The surface ceiling was 25,500 feet and the range 2,640 miles. Maximum bomb-load was 4,410 lbs which could be stowed internally or externally.

Dornier Do 17Z (known as the 'Flying Pencil')

Unlike the Heinkel 111, the Dornier 17 was a high-wing monoplane. Its crew were housed close together in the forward fuselage. Eight variants including a version known as the Dornier 215 were used during 1940-41 as Pathfinders, reconnaissance aircraft and bombers. Power was from two Bramo 323P radial engines each delivering 1000 h.p. or two Daimler Benz 601A-1 engines. Maximum speed was 265 m.p.h. with normal bomb-load. Surface ceiling was 26,740 feet, range 1,860 miles and a bomb-load of up to a maximum of 2,205 lbs.

Junkers Ju 88

The Ju 88 first flew in December 1936. It was probably the most versatile aircraft to serve the Luftwaffe. It served as a level-bomber, dive-bomber, night fighter and as a reconnaissance machine. It was used as a medium bomber against Liverpool but neither its speed nor its armament gave it adequate protection against the Spitfire or Hurricane.

Power units ranged from the Humo 211J and 213E to the BMW 801G engines, each delivering 1,200 h.p. Maximum speed 286 m.p.h. Ceiling height 26,500 feet, range normal 1,553 miles and bomb-load was gradually increased in the various marks to 5,510 lbs.

The start of the night bombing operations brought to the fore the activities of Kampfgruppe 100. This group pioneered the use of the Pathfinder technique.

Pathfinder aircraft generally operated over the target area at the height of 8,000 to 12,000 feet releasing flares and incendiary bombs, thus indicating the target area for the main bomber force which was usually positioned between 6,000 to 20,000 feet depending on the strength of the defences and the types of bombs to be used.

The German bomber flights were generally timed to arrive over their target areas at set intervals in order to confuse and disrupt the city's defences.

Two techniques were adopted for bombs to be released either by pre-arranged signal by the flight leader if a concentrated strike was to be made or it was left for individual bomb aimers to select their own targets.

Once the target was selected the bomb aimer sighted the target through a gyro-stabilized telescope which was operated by an electrical motor. Information was then fed into a sighting computer which had previously received detailed information of the bombs to be used and the altitude for release. The computer was also designed to give course corrections which were sited in front of the pilot. As the target area was approached, the Lofte 7D tachometric sighting telescrope moved to coincide with the angle given by the computer, simultaneously an electrical circuit released the bombs automatically.

Further aids to German pilots was a system called 'The Lorenz Beams' which was designed in 1938. It comprised of two adjacent radio beams which overlapped. One beam comprised of morse dots being transmitted, the other morse dashes. When the two beams overlapped a steady note was received. This simple method of radio navigation was known as Knickebein—'The Bent Leg'. It was mostly accurate, giving a crew a fifty per cent chance of placing their bombs within a one mile circle of the target. The virtue of Knickebein was its simplicity and it could be easily used by most bomber crews. These Knickebein transmitters were established at Stollberg on the west coast of Schleswig—Holstein, Cleve and at Lörrach in South-West Germany.

The Luftwaffe had two other aids for more precise bombing called X-*Gerät* and Y-*Gerät* (*Gerät* = device, apparatus). These developments were more complex which also employed the Lorenz Beams. The first was operated by Heinkel He 111 H-4S or KGr 100 Long-ranged bomber unit stationed at Vannes. The device consisted of 4 Radio frequencies (beams) each of which was transmitted on a different frequency. One, the approach beam, pointed at the target, the other three beams intercepted the approach beam at precise intervals. The first beam crossed the guiding one 30 miles from the target, there allowing the pilot to correct his course and set his aircraft up for the approach. The second beam was set at twelve miles from the target and the third at three miles, which set off a special clock, not unlike a stop-watch, but with two hands which rotated independently. At the three mile point, one hand which had been moving now stopped and the other hand started rotating to catch it up. When the two hands coincided, an electrical contact closed and the bombs were automatically released. This proved to be an efficient system but it could be and was jammed by the British.

A *Spitfire* (top) and a *Hurricane* - the two saviours of Britain in the fight against the *Luftwaffe,* and clear victors in the Battle of Britain.

The Bristol *Beaufighter* (from the same stable as the *Blenheim* and *Beaufort*) were interceptors of enemy bombers, both in daylight and at night.

The Dornier *Do17* bomber, which was extensively used by the Germans during the bombing of Britain.

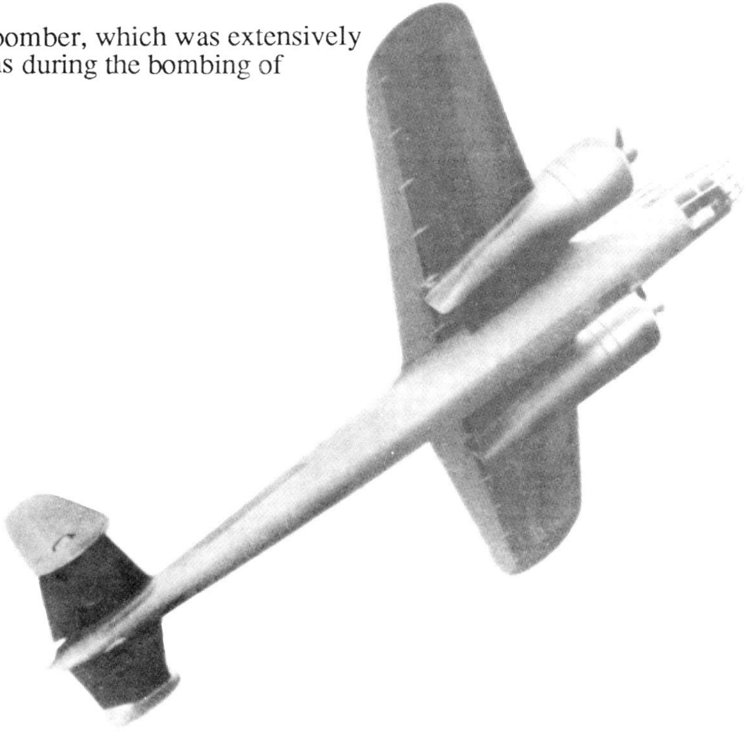

The Y-*Gerät* was more sophisticated. The point of release was determined by German ground radar stations using an interrogation pulse of 180 pulses a minute against a response signal from the aircraft. With this device an experienced crew could release their bombs within a circle four hundred yards in diameter when the aircraft was 180 miles from the home station. The Y-*Gerät* was however a more complex device which could only be used by specially trained personnel and eventually became ineffective once a suitable counter-measure had been worked out.

Transmitters were set up at Cherbourg and Cassel, Boulogne and Poix.

The British Answer

No. 12 Group of Fighter Command was ready—but only just ready—for battle. It was comprised mainly of Hurricanes and Spitfires, with the exception of two squadrons of Blenheims and one squadron of Defiants. The Hurricanes and Spitfires were reliable and had an excellent performance. Armed with eight machine guns they were superior in armament against the enemy bombers. The Spitfire in particular was fast, agile and manoeuverable. Its vital superiority was its fire power: eight wing-mounted guns held a decisive concentration of rounds per second, even though out-ranged by the bombers' cannons. Six squadrons of Spitfires defended the City. They were nos. 19, 64, 74, 266, 611 and 616.

The Hawker Hurricane, Britain's first monoplane fighter, was numerically the mainstay of Fighter Command during 1940. Although slower than the Spitfire, with a maximum speed of 328 m.p.h., the Hurricane was ideal as a bomber intercepter. Defending Hawker Hurricanes were squadrons 85, 151, 229, 242, 310 and a Polish squadron, No. 302.

The Boulton-Paul Defiant was less popular with the R.A.F. It was a two-seater fighter but not in the same class as the Spitfire and Hurricane, as it was slower, less agile, and armed with only four Browning machine-guns mounted in a power-operated turret. Boulton-Paul Defiant: squadron 264 was based at Kirton-in-Lindsey.

Towards the end of the blitz emerged the Bristol Beaufighter, a twin-engined night-fighter armed with six .303 machine-guns in the wings and four Hispano Cannon in the nose. Its maximum speed was 321 m.p.h. at 15,800 ft. Normal range 1,170 miles, service ceiling 26,500 ft.

The Blenheim 1F, nos. 23 and 29 squadron, a fighter version of the Blenheim Mk1 bomber, was a failure, but served as a stopgap night-fighter during the blitz. It was armed with one .303 machine-gun in the port wing, four .303 machine-guns in ventral fairing, one .303 Vickers K machine-gun in a hydraulically operated, semi-retractable dorsal turret. Its maximum speed was 285 m.p.h. at 15,000 ft., maximum range 1,125 miles, service ceiling 27,280 ft.

With these defences considerable success was achieved, but not enough to provide a deterrent: 2,750 people in the Liverpool area were killed, 2,548 seriously injured and 1,600 slightly injured.

June 1940

During an A.R.P. Exhibition held at Liverpool Central Station in 1938, a woman was overheard to say, "They will never get here and homb us, they couldn't get over the Pennines".

But two years later, shortly after midnight on June 25th, 1940, air raid sirens sounded for the first time in north-west England, and although planes were heard in the area and searchlights swept the clouds, there were no incidents, nor did the anti-aircraft defences go into action.

Two days later, on June 27th, aircraft were again heard over the area. Two bombs fell in a field, causing little damage. The following night, six bombs landed in a potato field.

July 1940

During the hours of darkness of July 2nd, 15th, 16th and 22nd enemy raiders again visited the Liverpool area. Two bombs were dropped on the 16th. One demolished the roof of a house in which eight people were sleeping. The only fatalities were two budgerigars.

In the early evening of July 24th, a lone raider was met by heavy anti-aircraft fire. No bombs were dropped, and it is believed the bomber, a Dornier, was brought down in the sea.

On the evening of July 29th, bombs were dropped harmlessly in fields around Irby, Neston and Thurstaston and near a searchlight site at Altcar.

August 1940

On August 1st, two bombs were dropped near the village of Halewood. One fell harmlessly in a field, the other in a cemetery among the dead. The damage was confined to several tombstones. But an A.R.P. Warden found, near the scene of the explosion, two dead thrushes, apparently killed by the blast. Inside one of the ten foot deep craters lay several dead rabbits.

At 12.30 a.m. on August 9th, a stick of six high explosive bombs fell on Birkenhead; one penetrated the roof of Mr. Bunney's house at Prenton, killing a maid; another fell in the middle of a roadway, blowing a garden wall askew and shattering windows in the vicinity. A further 20 bombs were dropped in surrounding fields causing no damage. The following night, August 10th, a stick of 11 high explosive bombs fell on Wallasey, where property was damaged by fire, water mains were fractured, and the railway embankment breached. Four people were killed and four were seriously injured!

August 13th and 14th again saw enemy bombers over the north-west area. Anti-aircraft defences were in action but no bombs were dropped.

In the early evening of August 15th two Heinkel 111 bombers made an attempt to reach the Liverpool area. As they crossed the coast they were intercepted by Hurricane fighters. One aircraft managed to escape into low cloud, with a fighter close on its tail. The other bomber was forced down into a field near Chester and was destroyed by its crew.

Fifteen bombs were dropped in a rural area of the north-west town in the early hours of the 16th August. Two farm houses escaped when high explosive bombs fell 39 yards away, smashing windows and destroying a hen coop, killing one chicken. The only other casualty, at a second farm, was a cow found dead in a field.

Just before midnight, August 17th, twenty parachutes, bearing official German markings were found in several parts of the north-west area. They contained no maps or documents and there was no evidence to show that they had been manned.

At 12.38 a.m. on 17th/18th August, 12 high explosive bombs were dropped on the Brunswick, North Coburg and South Queens Docks. A ship was overturned and a grain silo was damaged. Other bombs fell in the Caryl Street area, damaging the Overhead Railway and the L.M.S. Goods Station.

On the night of August 19th/20th, there was a sharp short raid by three enemy aircraft; the warning sirens sounded at 2.18 a.m. and the all-clear was given at 2.50 a.m. During this period, 100 incendiary bombs were reported to have been dropped, mainly in the Eaton Road district, where fire damage was caused to private houses and to the Robert Davies Nursing Home.

So brilliant was the greenish glow from the burning bombs that the glare could be seen five miles away; and at first, watchers had the impression that serious fires had started. But the material damage was remarkably light.

Eight nights later, on 27th August, enemy aircraft made a light attack on Wallasey. Firebombs were dropped: three fell harmlessly in fields, and the fourth damaged a water main. Meanwhile, at Liverpool, two bombs were dropped, damaging private houses. Near the scene, people were amused by a budgerigar shouting in its cage, through a window broken by the blast, "Here's those bloody planes again—down with Hitler!"

On August 28th, 150 enemy aircraft attacked Liverpool, Birkenhead and Wallasey. Many high-explosive and incendiary bombs were dropped on the City,with the exception of the centre area. Damage was mostly to residential and private property. Hundreds of incendiaries dropped harmlessly in fields and parklands, but a mansion was gutted, due to a lack of water pressure for the fire-fighters.

One bomb struck the south side of Mossley Hill Church, destroying most of the valuable stained-glass windows, wrecking the roof and part of the nave. Another bomb destroyed part of the churchyard wall, leaving a crater 10 feet wide. A pathetic witness to the time of the bombing was the church clock, which stopped. Two people were killed and a public service shelter was wrecked. A little girl was killed by a direct hit on an Anderson shelter on the Dovecot Estate.

The all-clear was sounded at 4.20 a.m.

200 bombers from 14 Gruppen, Dornier DO356 17Zs of KG 606 attacked Wallasey and Liverpool on the night of 30th/31st August. High-explosive and incendiary bombs were dropped on the Everton district of Liverpool. Mill Road Hospital was hit, and sheds at the Coburg Dock were damaged. Fire broke out in Sefton Street, and a man, woman and two children were killed when a bomb demolished their house in Brodie Avenue.

A Grammar School was also seriously damaged, and incendiary bombs damaged a farm, destroying bales of hay and straw. One raider was known to have been brought down by anti-aircraft fire.

September 1940

According to police reports there were three raids on Liverpool on the night of 31st August/1st September. The first was at 8.40 pm ending at 9.41 pm; the second was at 11.50 pm, ending at midnight; and the third started at two minutes past midnight, and went on until 3.10 am.

During these raids, serious damage was caused by high-explosive and incendiary bombs in the City, and over 100 small fires were reported. The Customs House was set on fire, two cotton warehouses were seriously damaged in Stone Street and Vandares Street. An air-raid shelter received a direct hit in Cleveland Square and an adjoining R.A.F. balloon site was completely destroyed, killing all the personnel.

Across the Mersey, Wallasey Town Hall was seriously damaged. There were many miraculous escapes during that night. One bomb fell in a front garden which had, a few days before, won a prize in the local 'Best Garden' competition, leaving a crater 5 feet in diameter; the front of the house was blown in but the occupants escaped uninjured. Their pet canary was blown completely out of its cage, unscathed and, after a few hours of freedom, was caught by a policeman and returned to its owner.

In another incident, a bomb actually dropped on the stone-wall of a cottage, at a road junction, at least half-a-mile from any other building. The occupier and his wife were in their Anderson shelter in the garden, and although the bomb dropped within ten feet of the shelter, they were not harmed. Nearby, a hen-coop was blown up and several cows were killed in a field.

One of the closest secrets of the war was the fact that the cruiser H.M.S. *Prince of Wales* was nearly sunk by an enemy bomb during a raid. Six bombs fell on Messrs. Cammell Laird's Shipyard; one dropped between the quayside and the *Prince of Wales*, which was lying berthed in the wet basin before she undertook her trials prior to being commissioned.

Blast from the bomb, which apparently exploded before it reached the bottom of the dock, burst open some of the cruiser's hull plates and she took on a list.

As efforts to secure the manhole lids failed, it was found that the tanks on the port side of the ship were also filling with water. In an effort to save her, the Birkenhead Fire Brigade was called, and pumps were quickly installed in the ship and on the quayside.

After two-and-a-half days work, during which workmen had to wade waist deep in water while plugging up holes and divers had to be sent down, the ship was saved. She was then removed to Dry-Dock for inspection and repair.

The *Prince of Wales*, which cost six million pounds, was later at the scene of the famous Atlantic Charter meeting between Mr. Roosevelt and Mr. Churchill, and she later took part in the destruction of the German battleship *Bismarck*. In December 1941, she was sunk off the east cost of Malaya by bombs of a Japanese aircraft.

On the night of September 3rd, the first warning the defences had of an impending enemy attack came at 9.57 pm. The attack took place at 11 pm, lasting seventeen minutes, but was followed immediately by a second attack which terminated at 3.43 am. During this time, wave after wave of bombers droned over the City, dropping parachute flares and showering hundreds of incendiary and high-explosive bombs down on the Kensington district, the Ullet Road area, Lark Lane and Aigburth Vale.

Incendiaries set fire to a Rope Works at Lodge Lane, and a girls High School at Aigburth Vale. Pollard's Garage (now Cubbin and North) was severely damaged. One fireman, dealing with a firebomb which had lodged in a roof close-by, was struck by another incendiary bomb which glanced off his steel helmet and fell onto the roadway below. The Palmyra Scent Works at Aigburth was also set on fire but the blaze was quickly under control.

At 9.58 pm on September 4th, the Liverpool sirens again sounded. At first little happened, but shortly after dark, waves of planes came over, attacking the Edge Hill and Lister Drive district. A number of hits were made on Edge Hill Goods Station and damage was done to Lister Drive Power Station; the Dunlop Rubber Works; the Tunnel Road Cinema, an ice-skating rink and a nearby billiards hall. A surface shelter, fire-station, and several schools and churches were also hit in the Green Lane area.

The following night, September 5th/6th, saw the introduction of a new type of German bomb. At 11.04 pm the now familiar menacing drone of bombers could be heard in the rain-filled sky. A few minutes before midnight, high-explosive and incendiary-bombs dropped on the Claudia Street, Walton area and Washington Street and St. James's Road were also badly damaged.

Crude oil-type bombs were used for the first time, causing extensive damage to houses. Everton Football Ground was struck by incendiary bombs, setting fire to seating accommodation. Six bombs missed the Cathedral, causing a ring of craters around the building. Some windows in the Lady Chapel were blown out and damage was done to the stone walls by bomb splinters.

At Birkenhead, a Children's Convalescent Home was hit, but there were no casualties. During daylight on September 6th, three 'purple' warnings were received by the Liverpool Control Centre. Planes were reported in the vicinity of the coast, but it was not until dusk was falling that the first attack was made.

At 8.31 pm five bombers could be clearly seen, flying high over the city; a few minutes later, high explosive and incendiary bombs set fire to the Liverpool Grease, Oil and Chemical Company works at Norfolk Street. The glow from the fire was so intense that people could see it at the end of the city.

Later in the night, bombs fell in the Milner Safe Works at Smithdown Lane, damaging 14 A.R.P. ambulances.

A few minutes before midnight, a bomb struck the Cathedral, glancing off the roof and falling into Founders Plot. Damage was done to the outer fabric of the south wall, which was gashed by flying stones and bomb splinters. The bomb also dislodged a few blocks of stone at the foot of the steps leading to the Lady Chapel, causing only slight damage. The damage to some of the stained-glass windows was, however, more serious. In fact most of the glass in the windows along half the length of the south wall was destroyed, as well as all the windows in the Lady Chapel facing Founders Plot.

All the 'Famous Women' windows were blown in and in the choir, the Ruby and Emerald windows were shattered. Some of the Vestry windows were holed and in the south choir aisle, the Annexe window was blown out.

A curious feature was that no portion of the uncompleted part of the Cathedral had a window damaged, although bombs dropped less than 50 yards away demolished a dozen houses.

On the night of 10th/11th September, some damage was done and the attack appeared to be widespread. At 10.08 pm raiders attacked West Derby and the Woolton district with high-explosive bombs. Houses were severely damaged in the Speke area, and three unexploded bombs dropped in a field near Deysbrook Lane anti-aircraft site. At Waterloo a bomb destroyed a farm building and a large shippon. A silo, built only the day before, was completely destroyed. Several bombs fell on the Woolton golf course, and at Crosby and Litherland several houses were wrecked, but no casualties were caused.

The night of September 11th/12th saw a short, sharp raid that started at 10.10 pm and ended at 12.45 am. Oil, incendiary and high-explosive bombs were dropped on the Gateacre area, and a 300 year old farm received damage: the occupants had a narrow escape as the house swayed from side to side when five bombs fell close by. At a nearby farm a small fire merely destroyed an out-building, and at a third, corn was destroyed.

A little boy five years old was killed when an incendiary bomb fell through the roof into his bedroom, on the night of September 12th/13th in a two-hour raid. Serious damage was done to buildings around the south-west Langton Dock. Two houses were destroyed in Wellington Road, Wavertree, and a large private house was damaged by fire in Carnatic Road, Aigburth.

During a nine-minute raid on September 14th, a single raider dropped high-explosive and incendiary-bombs, causing slight damage to the Gladstone and Alexandra Docks.

Intense anti-aircraft fire caused raiders on the night of September 15th/16th to drop their bombs at random and flee. In the late evening, enemy aircraft approached the area, attacking mainly the Anfield, Fairfield, Walton and Norris Green districts. Bombs also landed on Speke Airport but caused little damage. The Palace Ice Rink was again severely damaged (disproving the popular superstitition that 'lightning doesn't strike the same place twice') and a house in Huntley Road was demolished. A singular feature of the raid was the total absence of incendiary bombs.

A Dornier DO215 of AUF KL GR 123 was intercepted and chased by a Spitfire of 266 Squadron. It was later shot down over the island of Walcheren.

At noon on the 16th, a delayed-action bomb exploded, killing the entire bomb disposal team that had been working on it since early morning. The raiders returned later in the same day dropping bombs and causing extensive damage in Great Homer Street, killing an Auxiliary Fireman. Incendiary bombs also landed on the Carlton Cinema, Moss Lane, during a performance.

Among all the anguish, the horror and bravery, there were many light-hearted moments which the Scouser's inbuilt humour exploited to the full. For example, one incendiary bomb fell down the chimney of a private house, setting alight papers and wood which had been placed in the grate a few minutes earlier. The occupants of the house were in their Anderson shelter and on returning to the house, found the fire lit—the magnesium bomb having burnt itself out in the proper place without so much as damaging carpet or furniture.

The following day, the 17th September, again saw the viciousness of the Nazis. At 3.06 pm, raiders swept over Liverpool making what appeared to be a reconnaisssance flight. Later at 7.48 pm they returned in force, bombing Garston and Speke and narrowly missing the Rootes aircraft (formerly motor-car) factory. Widespread and severe damage was caused when bombs landed on houses in the Lockerby Road area; and at Green Lane, Old Swan, a bomb demolished a house, killng eight A.F.S. firemen.

At Currie Street, a policeman was fatally injured. At 8.51 pm through clouds of smoke and dust the all-clear could be heard, but not for long. Two hours later,. at 10.12 pm, twenty enemy raiders were reported, flying fast and low towards the city. But it was to be Wallasey's turn. Extensive damage was done to houses and there were many casualties. A bomb struck an A.F.S post killing all the occupants. Firemen from a nearby station had turned into one street, when a high-explosive bomb fell at a road junction they had just passed. These same men were later machine-gunned by a low-flying plane as they helped to rescue trapped people from a blazing house.

Heavy damage throughout the whole of Liverpool was reported by the police on the 18th/19th September. The raid began at 5.41 pm and ended at 1.05 am. Walton Prison received a direct hit from a high-explosive bomb trapping several people. Railway lines were damaged at Brownlow Hill and St. Michael's Station, Aigburth. Work had to be stopped at the A.T.M. Company Works at Old Swan due to an unexploded bomb and a Nurses' Home at Fazakerley Hospital was damaged. As usual, schools, shops, hotels and houses suffered most from high-explosive and incendiary bombs. Over 1,000 high-explosive bombs and 500 incendiaries were dropped.

People saw five raiders challenged by a British fighter. One aircraft broke away and headed toward the sea with smoke pouring from one of its engines.

During the afternoon of September 19th, a lone German raider penetrated the area without dropping bombs, and at 7.32 pm a light bomber force made four passes over the city, the Walton, Anfield and West Derby districts receiving most of the damage. Houses in Hillary Road and Rossmore Gardens, West Derby, were severely damaged and an anti-aircraft gun site had to be evacuated when an unexploded bomb landed near one of the guns.

The following day, September 20th, no enemy aircraft were reported over the north-west area, but on the night of the 21st/22nd there were two raids lasting until 4.21 am. During the first attack much damage was done, but in the second attack twenty bombers concentrated on the central area of the City. The department store of T.J. Hughes, London Road, was seriously damaged by a high-explosive bomb. Central Station and the Mersey Underground were penetrated, seriously damaging two trains. Large fires broke out in the warehouses of the Alexandra Dock and at Byng Street. A timber yard in Rimrose Road was set on fire. The East Lancashire Road, Lowerhouse Lane, London Road and Stretford Street were closed by rubble and bomb craters.

One Dornier DO215 was shot down at Dolgellau, North Wales by a fighter from 611 Squadron.

A single German aircraft was sighted flying high over the river at 10.30 am on the 23rd September, but was driven off by heavy anti-aircraft fire before it could drop its bombs on the city. But later in the evening, the first of three attacks took place at 7.05 pm. Bootle, which from the raiders' point of view counted as part of Liverpool, suffered considerable damage. At 10.23 pm the second attack was centred on the Walton area. A church and a chapel and numerous tomb stones at Walton Park Cemetery were damaged. The final attack was made at 12.23 am in which incendiaries and 'Molotov Bread Baskets' were used for the first time. The church in Robson Street was damaged by an incendiary bomb; a few nights earlier it had received a direct hit by high-explosives, damaging the organ and smashing the valuable stained-glass windows.

Twenty minutes before the all-clear was given at 4.09 am, a bright flash was seen in the sky; it was believed that a large calibre bomb had been exploded in mid-air by anti-aircraft shell fragments.

After a quiet night, the Germans changed their attack times from the usual 7 pm—midnight to the early morning. At 2.50 am on the 24th/25th, the sirens wailed as the menacing throb of planes could be heard in the distance.

At 3.10 am the enemy attacked, using a new method to avoid the anti-aircraft batteries; silently they glided down with engines turned off in order to make a moonlight hit-and-run raid on the city centre. Little damage was done and there were no casualties. Later, a second wave of bombers arrived, striking at the heart of the city and causing serious damage to warehouses in Clegg Street. The Stanley Tobacco Warehouse and Silcocks Cattle Food Mill at Great Howard Street and Love Lane received direct hits.

Shops in Parker Street, Clayton Square and Church Street were set on fire. A woman patient at a mental hospital escaped death by inches when a large piece of anti-aircraft shell penetrated the roof, went through a bed occupied by a woman on the top floor, in between two beds on the second floor, then on to the third. All escaped uninjured. Such stories of miraculous escapes formed part of the everyday conversation of the Liverpudlians, although morale remained high and scare-stories tended to be disbelieved.

A new type of magnesium bomb was dropped during the raid. One was found by wardens, buried in the front garden of a house; using two pieces of wood paling as a spade, they managed to dig it out without its exploding. It is believed that twenty of these bombs were dropped.

At 5 pm on the evening of 26th/27th September, people standing at the Pier Head watched the balloon barrage ascend into the evening sky like silver sausages. Little did they realise how much they were going to owe to those 'gasbags', some two hours later. At 7.23 pm aircraft were seen heading at a great speed towards Liverpool. The sound of the sirens had hardly died away when the first formation of Heinkel 111s streaked over the coast at New Brighton. For some minutes 'hedge-hopping' the balloons, the first two aircraft machine-gunned the balloons in an effort to clear the way for those following behind. Three balloons caught fire, but the barrage remained solid and forced the raiders to fly higher.

Many foolhardy people of Liverpool stood in the main streets that evening, cheering and ignoring the danger from falling bombs as they watched anti-aircraft shells bursting round the centre plane of a group of five. The aircraft appeared to receive a direct hit, losing height, and it is believed to have crashed in the Mersey estuary where it remains buried to this day. It seemed that the first wave of aircraft was intent on starting fires to act as beacons for those expected in the area after dark. At 10.40 pm, the second and heavier formation of bombers arrived, doing extensive damage to the Wapping, King's, Queen's, Coburg and Brunswick Docks. Thirteen warehouses were seriously damaged and the Admiralty Stores in Canning Place were destroyed.

The Mersey Docks and Harbour Board Offices and Cunard Buildings in Brunswick Street were hit by high-explosive bombs, and the tug *Wellington* was severely damaged at the King's Dock. In spite of much brave news to the contrary, the German bombers were often far more accurate in their bombing than was officially admitted at the time.

Many oil-bombs and 'Molotov Bread Baskets' were dropped, causing large fires; At one Government office, thousands of Income Tax records were completely destroyed (to the barely suppressed glee of those who knew of the incident) and the nearby Public Assistance Office was seriously damaged.

At Birkenhead, the famous Argyll Theatre received a direct hit by an incendiary-bomb. After burning its way through the roof, the bomb set fire to the auditorium, balcony and dressing rooms. The whole building was burnt down except for the office (which contained many of the original programmes and bills of over 90 years ago), and the foyer, where historic old-time photographs hung on the walls.

The following night, 27th/28th September, the raiders made another sharp, short visit to the port. There were three attacks in quick succession in the space of one hour. Houses were demolished in the Great Homer Street area, and the council school at Banks Road, Garston was damaged.

The main areas attacked on the 29th/30th September were the Dingle, Aigburth and Everton districts. The raid started at 10 pm: only a few high-explosive bombs were dropped, but the large number of incendiaries caused serious fires. The Hamlet Free Church at Aigburth was struck by an oil-bomb and was completely gutted. Nearby in the Mayfair Cinema, members of the audience were unaware of the imminent danger of the building catching fire because of the intense heat from the burning church. One hundred yards from the church, the Aigburth Public Library was set on fire but was saved by the prompt action of the Fire Service.

Two firemen were killed by a falling wall while fighting fires at the Duke's Dock, where highly inflammable oil-cake, flax and grain warehouses were set alight by incendiaries.

Six hours later—at 4 am—the all-clear was given but raging fires still lit the sky.

Earlier in the same day, nine Hurricane fighters had saved Liverpool from what might have been a serious daylight bombing. It was about 6.30 am when the Hurricanes, on patrol over the Irish Channel, sighted a formation of nine Heinkel bombers roughly midway between St. David's Head and Rosslare in Ireland. The Heinkels were flying fast and high to the north-east which would have taken them into the Liverpool area. The Hurricanes attacked at once; immediately the Heinkels veered towards the west until one crashed into the sea near Wexford, Eire. Two bombers were badly damaged and it was unlikely that they reached France. Three Hurricanes were lost in this action.

By the end of September, Liverpool and the rest of Merseyside could truly say that they had had their real baptism of fire. It could be argued that the night of November 28th/29th was the first serious, full-scale attack on the port, but the casualty figures for the month of September indicated how extremely serious the situation was: 277 persons had been killed and 484 seriously injured.

October 1940

October 1940 came, and with it a short, sharp attack on the port at 7.35 pm. Raiders were seen forming up over the sea, no doubt determined to press home and attack immediately after dusk. However, they were quickly dispersed by a flight of Hurricanes who forced them to jettison their bombs into the sea. Two enemy aircraft managed to evade the fighters, dropping incendiary bombs on the East Toxteth Dock

Three persons were killed and a number seriously injured when bombs destroyed a row of shops and severely damaged a cinema at Kensington on 2nd October.

Raiders evaded the Liverpool anti-aircraft defences on October 3rd and concentrated their attention on the Manchester and Salford areas. Although it was the largest raid of the war that the two cities had experienced, in which a large number of bombs were dropped, there was surprisingly little damage and few casualties were sustained.

During a sharp raid on Liverpool on the 4th October, a Liverpool Corporation bus was attacked as it sped along the main road at Speke. Prompt action by the driver saved the lives of his passengers. In an eye-witness account he said:

> "My conductor shouted that a plane was coming very low down behind us, but I had already heard the clatter of anti-aircraft guns and observed that the plane was dropping low; then I heard the rattle of his machine-gun and immediately swerved to the opposite side of the road".

An A.F.S. Fireman who was walking along the same road at the time had a lucky escape when a bullet knocked off his cap.

At 8 pm on the 7th/8th October, bombers returned after three nights' absence. Damage to houses was severe in Stanley Road, Great Mersey Street, Lichfield Road and the Wavertree area. A Welsh Chapel was destroyed in Great Mersey Street. The raiders appeared to take full advantage of the low cloud and bad weather, which earlier in the day had prevented the use of the balloon barrage. The attacks came in small waves or else as single machines which had broken away from the main bomber force attacking the Manchester area.

Members of the RAF examine a shot-down *Junkers 88* for valuable information about armaments and equipment.

Mrs Irene Cheshire and friend, of Verdi Street, Crosby (near the North Docks), defiantly drape the union jack outside their damaged home, October 1940.

Officials inspect Liverpool Stadium after the raid of 12/13th March 1941.

Large numbers of incendiary bombs were dropped around Aigburth, most of which burned themselves out in Sefton Park. A hospital, a laundry and a Church of England Infant School were badly damaged by high-explosive bombs.

At one house, a budgerigar was blown out of its cage over the top of a settee and picked up alive.

The following day, 9th October, a lone Junkers 88 bomber took advantage of the rain clouds and attacked Garston and Aigburth. As it appeared suddenly out of the clouds, anti-aircraft batteries on both sides of the River Mersey put up an intensive barrage. At the same time, a British and two Czech pilots were waiting for the enemy and by clever manoeuvering prevented the Junkers from reaching the protection of the clouds. The aircraft was chased across the river and eventually burst into flames on making a belly-landing near Eastham Docks. One member of the crew was killed, another injured, and two surrendered.

Shortly after dark on the 10th October, Royal Observer Corps observers reported heavy bombers heading towards Liverpool. Incendiary bombs fell at Knotty Ash, Mossley Hill and Kirkdale. The raid lasted just over an hour. At 9.36 pm two hours later, the enemy returned, causing damage to a childrens' sanatorium, the Ritz Roller Skating Rink at Catherine Street, and severely damaged houses in Everton Valley and Mill Street. Serious damage was caused at Marmingham Road, Anfield and Hogarth Road, Kirkdale.

A bomb was seen by workmen to bounce off the side of a bus, pass under a glass verandah and disappear through a shop window.

On the night of 11th October, it appeared that the enemy was intent from the start on attacking the dock area. At 6.30 pm, the first of the two raids was made. Two hospitals, a convent, a home for the aged and a cinema all narrowly escaped serious damage. The cinema was full of people when it was straddled by three high-explosive bombs. It was thought there were twelve aircraft in the first flight, mostly of the Dornier type.

People all over the city witnessed a 'dog fight' between a German bomber and a Hurricane fighter. The enemy was later shot down into the sea off West Kirby.

During the second raid, a heavy bomber force of Dorniers attacked the city and north docks. Severe damage was caused at South John Street, James Street, Red Cross Street, Paradise Street, Hanover Street and South Castle Street. Serious damage was also caused to dock sheds, the Harbour Master's House, four ships and the Alexandra and Langton Docks.

Admiralty and railway stores were destroyed at Hill Street and Bank Hall Street. One bomb made a direct hit on a school.

A man was severely injured whilst dealing with an incendiary bomb; he was putting soil on the bomb when a person threw a brick on it causing the burning fragments to fly up into his face.

It was officially announced that three Dornier bombers were destroyed in the two raids.

More than forty enemy bombers attacked Liverpool on the night of the 13th/14th October. For four hours the aircraft circled the fringe of the anti-aircraft barrage, taking individual turns to dart in through a temporary break.

There were many instances of coolness and courage when two heavy high-explosive bombs struck the opposite ends of a large block of tenements at Myrtle Gardens, where eleven people were killed and nine seriously injured. Private houses were also damaged at Gadsby Street, Everton, and fires broke out in dock sheds at the North Hornby and Gladstone Docks.

The following day, no attacks were made on the port but during the early afternoon of the 16th, a single reconnaissance plane was seen high over the city. Later, at 7.24 pm, five Heinkel 111s attacked the city, dropping their bombs at random. A church at Everton was destroyed by incendiaries and a brewery and a block of flats received direct hits by high-explosive bombs.

One stick of bombs fell on Mere Lane, Everton, causing many casualties. Two surface shelters in Louisa Street were destroyed.

In a brief raid on the 17th, extensive damage was caused to a hospital, two schools and private houses in the West Derby area. The west wing of Fazakerley Sanatorium was demolished, killing a patient; and in the Smithdown Road area, an unexploded bomb was found in the yard of the Morrison School.

In the late evening of October 18th, heavy damage was caused by high-explosive bombs in the Norris Green area and in the southern part of the city. St. Clement's church, Beaumont Street, was seriously damaged.

On the night of the 19th, St. Silas' Church, Dingle, and the Seamans' Orphanage, Orphan Drive were damaged; and a heavy unexploded bomb was found in Newsham Park. Tuebrook and the Dingle appeared to be the areas mostly attacked and severe damage was caused in High Park Street.

October 20th was a mainly quiet day, but three planes passed over the south end of the city. Bombs were dropped in fields and on a roadway but no casualties were caused.

In an eight-hour raid starting at 6.58 pm on October 21st, severe damage was caused by incendiary bombs over a wide area of the city. Houses in Dacy Road and Breck Road were destroyed, and two tram cars were damaged in Priory Road, Anfield.

An aerial-type mine (Type G) caused extensive damage to water mains at Aigburth Vale.

On the 22nd of the month, a single bomber dropped a bomb near a cinema, killing two boys and two girls as they were buying their tickets.

On October 23rd, Liverpool had its 200th alert since the blitz began. It was the longest single raid of the war, lasting ten hours, but little damage was caused and casualties were light.

On the 24th, reconnaissance aircraft were seen twice during the day. No bombs were dropped.

On the 25th, twenty-five planes were seen, but again no bombs fell. Later, at 7.33 pm, a light bomber force headed in from the Irish Sea, bombing the Richmond Park area. Houses were destroyed, serious damage was caused to Holy Trinity School and a fire broke out at Mill Lane Rope Works.

A five-hour raid on the night of the 26th/27th brought severe damage to houses in the Netherfield Road area. Sixteen people were trapped when fire broke out, impeding rescue work. There were few survivors.

In the same district, an ARP section-post was demolished, killing a warden and seriously injuring another. One unusual feature of this raid was that 'screaming bombs' were introduced for the first time. Their purpose was to terrorise the civilian population—but the ruse failed. Very soon folk-wisdom improvised the counter-ploy, "If you can hear them coming you know they won't hit you". Like so much benevolent, defensive propaganda, it was not strictly true. But those best able to refute it did not, alas, usually survive to tell the tale.

By the 28th October it was quite clear that the Germans were increasing their attention on the Merseyside port installations. On the 29th, the 'purple' warning was flashed to all commands, and at 6 pm a 'red' warning was given. For four hours nothing happened. But at midnight reports of the first incidents were coming in. Fires broke out in sheds at the North-East Queens Dock; an AFS post at the Queens Dock was destroyed, killing its occupants. A public house opposite the dock gates was severely damaged. That night many bombs fell on the dock-estate and surrounding houses.

An amazing story was told by Mr. Atkinson whose house was destroyed during the raid.

> "My wife and I were sheltering under the stairs when an explosive bomb rocked the house. We were covered n dust as articles fell on us. I was hurled across the pantry by the blast and, on getting up, felt something trickling down my face. Thinking it was blood, I shouted to my wife, "Oh, Alice, my head has gone . . ."
> "Yes" interrupted his wife, laughing, "when I shone my torch on his face, it was covered in caster oil".
> ". . . a bottle from the shelf must have fallen on me"!

In a police report on the 29th/30th October, it was recorded that three daylight warnings took place. The first two passed without incident but the third saw severe damage to warehouses in Thomas Street and South Castle Street. The telephone exchange at South John Street was temporarily interrupted and incendiary bombs showered down on Bold Street. At the south end of the city, the match factory of Bryant and May, Garston, was itself set alight—an easy victim to incendiary bombs; and a railway siding at Speke was also set on fire.

Casualties for October were 136 killed and 167 seriously injured.

November 1940

Defence Headquarters were alerted at 7.46 pm on the 1st, as bombers crossed the coast. Incendiaries fell on County Road, Great Howard Street and the East Lancashire Road area.

There were three incidents on the night of the 4th/5th November, the raids lasting until 4 am. Bombs were dropped at random on Townsend Avenue and Wavertree Playground, where a gas-main caught fire.

On the 6th November it was officially and apparently accurately announced that the combined efforts of anti-aircraft and RAF defences had accounted for the destruction of 17 enemy aircraft. This total did not include those raiders damaged and which may have been forced into the sea. But it must be said that reports of lost enemy aircraft always erred on the optimistic side, without necessarily spreading intentional propaganda untruths. It often heppened that several fighter pilots found themselves credited with the same kill. And anti-aircraft batteries which fired on an aircraft would perhaps not be aware that it had already been hit (and claimed) by another battery.

During the night of the 8th/9th November, there were six short alerts. But the only incident occurred during the period 7.50 - 8 pm when incendiaries were dropped on Childwall Valley Road district.

November 10th/11th. Liverpool was attacked by 22 aircraft from *Küstenfliegergruppe* 606 (i.e. the German equivalent of Coastal Command). One of their aircraft was shot down.

On the 12th November, Edge Hill Railway Goods Station and surrounding districts were severely attacked. One oil incendiary bomb fell on the roof of the Post Office in Wavertree Road, causing slight damage; and because of high winds the balloon barrage was unable to operate, thereby giving the bombers the advantage of being able to fly at low altitude.

On November 14th, aircraft were reported in the vicinity of Merseyside but there were no incidents.

On the 15th, twelve bombs were dropped in a rural area. No damage was caused.

At 2.52 a.m. on the 18th, during a thunderstorm, incendiaries struck houses in Guest Street and warehouses in Sefton Street. A number of balloons were set on fire by the lightning.

On the night of the 19th, four young children and their 84-year-old grandmother were killed when a bomb hit their house.

Many incendiaries and high explosive bombs were dropped on Aigburth where dwelling houses, shops and a church were extensively damaged. A church school at Aigburth Vale and houses at 3 and 5 Wyngate Road were destroyed.

Three houses in Tenlon Street, Anfield, were demolished during the same raid.

On the night of the 20th/21st, bombs were dropped in fields. No serious damage.

On the 23rd November, shortly after midnight six sailors were taken by surprise when a lone raider, gliding in with its engines shut off, dropped two bombs on Great George Street. The seamen were blown through the front of a lock-up shop and three of them were killed instantly. The other three were seriously injured.

At 7.03 p.m. on November 28th, a 'purple' warning was received at defence headquarters. It was immediately flashed to all anti-aircraft sights and the R.A.F.

At 7.23 p.m. the siren sounded and within a few minutes people realised that this was no ordinary raid. Wave after wave of bombers headed up the river, dropping their heavy loads of incendiary and high-explosive bombs over a wide area. For the first time the population experienced the devastation and terror caused by parachute mines as these drifted silently and stealthily to earth. With them, the saying reported earlier about the 'screaming bombs' came uncomfortably close to the truth.

The police report on the raid was as follows:

> "The raid commenced with incendiary bombs, followed by high-explosive and parachute mines on Britannic Park and Durning Road, where a basement shelter was hit. Damage was also caused to Rose Place and district. A parachute mine landed on Commercial Road causing serious damage to house property. Parachute mines were also responsible for fire and damage to Spofforth Road Gas Works, and a shed containing sugar at Garston docks. Serious damage was done in Holland Street and Ardleigh Road. Allerton, Wavertree and Childwall districts were heavily bombed with incendiaries and at least thirty parachute mines were dropped in these areas, eight of which failed to explode."

The attack on Liverpool on the 29th November was, at that time, the longest and most severe yet experienced by the city. The cost of life and material damage was very heavy.

During the raid, Garston Gas Works was attacked. At 3 a.m. the pressureman on duty reported that No. 1 Holder was descending rapidly. This gas-holder (of four million cubic feet capacity) was, at the time, about half-full. The pressureman took immediate action by shutting off the holder from service and notified the responsible officials of the incident. Members of the duty breakdown squad were immediately despatched to the gasworks. It must be emphasised that the type of bomb that had entered the holder was not known; the only indication of its nature was obtained when, in pitch darkness, crawling across the crown of the holder, employees making for the manhole felt a piece of fabric protruding from the sheeting.

At 7.30 a.m. fitters and electricians, plumbers and others were at work disconnecting electrically driven blowers from other plants and rigging them in position in the holder; and preparing the fire pump to draw water from the bottom. The tasks were carried out by willing volunteers. As the exact location of the bomb had not been known, risks had to be taken.

Firstly, the fans were started up and nothing happened; then the motor pump and still nothing blew up. The men who had assembled the gear were withdrawn, except one to watch the running of the job. Three of the attendants worked in relays round the clock.

The Liverpool Fire Brigade arrived and put a pump to work; the water was taken down to five feet, to uncover a lot of the dimpling which formed a brick-faced island inside the holder.

This achieved, and the air inside the holder being considered non-explosive and fit to breathe, means of access were discussed. Efforts to see the 'culprit' through the manholes with the aid of portable searchlights were unsuccessful and it was decided to cut a hole in the crown of the holder from which a ladder could be landed on the mud-covered 'dimpling' cover, to enable Naval Mine Disposal personnel to enter and defuse the suspected parachute mine.

By means of oxy-acetylene-cutting gear, a hole about six feet square was cut; fans and pumps were stopped and the job was handed over to the Naval Officers. Donning oxygen apparatus, Lieutenant Newgass entered the holder. He lashed the parachute ring of the mine to the top of the pillar against which the mine was found to be leaning, and passed a lashing round the nose of the mine to prevent its slipping onto the floor.

He also placed some sandbags around the nose. Unfortunately the fuse was facing the pillar so a special hoisting lug was affixed and the mine was turned with a long tommy-bar—a great physical effort for one man wearing oxygen apparatus for the first time.

The fuse, magnetic primer and the clockwork removed, the keep-ring being extremely stiff, Lieutenant Newgass then left the holder and reported that although the detonator was still in, the mine could be considered reasonably safe. He had been in the holder for three hours except for short periods of rest and to obtain refills of oxygen. His cool and outstanding courage earned Lieutenant Howard Reginald Newgass the George Cross.

An Air Ministry communique laconically stated:

> "There was considerable activity over this country on the 28th/29th November and, although a large number of bombs were dropped in various districts, the main weight of the attack was directed against the north-west of England and particularly against Merseyside".

But the Nazi press described it more graphically—and, for once, alas, all too accurately:

> "Huge fires in the Liverpool area are reported by bomber crews returning from a large scale raid throughout the night. Mile long fires were seen to be raging in the grain elevators, oil mills, docks and oil depots and aircraft factories on Merseyside".

They omitted, of course, to mention another outcome of the mass raid—the destruction of a large basement shelter under the Junior Technical School at Durning Road.

A cleaner, who was employed there, gave this eye-witness account:

> "I was one of the regulars at the shelter with my little boy and girl. There were 250 of us in the girls' section and about 150 in the boys'. Earlier in the night, two tramcars pulled up in front of the shelter and a lot of people came down. Then, during the first part of the raid, the surface shelter was hit and two people were killed. All those who were uninjured flocked down to our part—they were not refused admission. We were packed like sardines. Most of the visitors had gone into the inner section. Then came an explosion and the lights went out.
>
> The A.R.P. Warden told us it was the blast from the nearby bomb, and I could hear the glass crashing down above us. Then a few minutes later came the big one. The noise was terrific. The roof split open and came crashing down on us, covering us with debris. Very few were hurt in our section, but in the boiler room and other parts, fire broke out and many must have been killed on the spot."

Sixty of those trapped were rescued alive, but 180 others were killed in that incident alone. The raid lasted seven-and-a-half hours.

The following night, a lone raider was driven off by the ground defences as soon as it had dropped its load of incendiary and high-explosive bombs on the Rathbone Road area.

During the month, civilian casualties were 316 killed and 202 seriously injured.

December 1940

For three weeks the Liverpool area was free from attacks. Light raids were, however, made on the 2nd, 5th, 12th, 13th, 16th and 19th December. On each occasion no damage was caused and it seemed that the aircraft were on reconnaissance flights.

At 6.20 p.m. on December 20th, 50 bombers of KU FL GR 606 raided the city for nine-and-a-half hours. It was an intensive attack in which many incendiary, high-explosive bombs and parachute mines were dropped.

Extensive fires raged along the docks and incendiary bombs fell on the Town Hall, Municipal Buildings and the Cunard offices at the Pier Head. Nine men were killed when a parachute mine landed on Waterloo Dock.

At Copperas Hill, a mine narrowly missed the Adelphi Hotel. Warehouses in Dublin Street were set on fire and Exchange Station was closed. At Bentinck Street five railway arches were hit. These arches were used as unofficial shelters and, at the time of the attack, ninety people were huddled together under the structure. The bomb landed on the middle arch which collapsed, hurling huge concrete blocks onto the people below. It took five days to complete the rescue of forty-eight people but forty-two lost their lives.

The next night, December 21st, 150 bombers of KU FL GR 606 made their appearance at 6.38 p.m. The weight of the attack came in two waves—from 7 p.m. to 10.40 p.m., and from midnight until 5.15 a.m. Parachute mines, high-explosive bombs and firebombs rained down on the city. This raid was even bigger and more serious than that of the preceding night had been. Five aircraft were shot down, three by fighters and two by anti-aircraft fire.

The North docks were seriously damaged, notably the Canada, Gladstone, Brocklebank, Princess, Wapping, King's and Carriers, where warehouses were set on fire and the walls badly damaged.

Serious damage was done to the Fish Market, Hatton Garden and an electric station at Highfield Street. At Hanover Street, the chemical firm of Ayrton Saunders received a direct hit by a high-explosive bomb and severe damage was done to Goodlass Wall (Paint Works). At Prescot Street, a police station received damage from a parachute mine, and a bedding factory close by was destroyed. A parachute mine caused damage to the Liverpool Royal Infirmary in Pembroke Place, and demolished dwelling-houses in the same area.

St. George's Hall and the Assize Court were set on fire and precautionary measures had to be taken by the police to evacuate hundreds of people in a large shelter below the building.

A 'Molotov Bread-Basket' completely destroyed a church and heavy bombs demolished a row of houses. At the Gaiety Cinema, several people who stayed in the building for shelter were killed when a high-explosive bomb blew off the roof.

Double-decker buses were destroyed when a bomb fell on a bus depot. At Roe Street a fire engine urgently responding to a call drove into a bomb crater, killing its crew of seven men.

The Leeds-Liverpool canal was breeched when a delayed-action bomb exploded, bursting the banks. A coal barge moored nearby was swept through the breech, ending up in a nearby railway goods yard.

St. Anthony's School, St. Alphonsus Church and the Crescent Church were severely damaged and the Royal Navy establishment at Melia's Building, Love Lane, was destroyed; and it appeared that parachute mines were used extensively during this raid.

On the 23rd December, Liverpool suffered a light attack starting at 6.38 p.m. until 6.12 a.m. During the raid, high-explosive and incendiary bombs caused serious damage to 7 and 9 Medlock Street. Six people were killed by a bomb at a garage in Ensor Street. Damage was caused at No. 2 Huskisson Dock Shed and a man was killed when a ship was hit by a bomb in the Canada Tongue Dock.

The Langton and Alexandra Docks were slightly damaged. At Speke, the motor car factory of Messrs. Rootes Ltd. received a direct hit from a high-explosive bomb which demolished a shelter, killing one person and seriously injuring three others.

In the same night, Manchester, Salford and Stretford were also fiercely attacked with incendiary bombs; and without doubt, December 23rd was also Manchester's night of endurance. Shortly after dusk, the main bomber force split from those attacking Liverpool. They paid special attention to Stretford, where large fires were started. Serious damage was caused to Oxford Road and the Deansgate area of Manchester. It was estimated that 150 enemy aircraft were over the two cities during the 22nd and 23rd of December, and that 356 civilians lost their lives. During the same night, a Home for Women at Wallasey was destroyed. There were few survivors, as those trapped beneath the debris were suffocated by a broken gas main as they lay helpless under the rubble.

One bomber was shot down over Sussex and another over Blackpool.

The following night was Christmas Eve, but there was no let-up. Raiders were reported over the area at 7.08 p.m. High-explosive bombs fell in the river opposite the Brunswick Half-Tide dock, but this time little damage and casualties resulted, and the raid ended at 1.23 a.m. on Christmas Day.

On the morning of 27th December the Isle of Man steamer *Victoria* was outward-bound and about eight miles north-west of the Bar Lightship when she struck a mine which left her helpless. For some hours H.M.Y. *Evadne* stood by until the trawler *Michael Griffiths* managed to get a line on the stricken ship and eventually towed her back to the Mersey for repairs.

The final attack of the year came on the 28th December, when a single enemy aircraft was sighted during the afternoon. Anti-aircraft defences went into action and the plane was driven off.

January 1941

For the next two weeks there was a blessed lull in really concentrated bombing. Bombs did, however, fall on No. 11 Red Cross Street and a block of offices. Warehouses was seriously damaged in Mercer Court on the 1st January, just to see the New Year in on an appropriately ominous note.

During the same raid, a heavy calibre bomb was reported to have been dropped in the river near the Brunswick Dock entrance and a suspected parachute mine caused serious damage to warehouses near the same dock.

Two nights later on the 3rd January, a single aircraft dropped incendiary bombs on the Sandforth Road district and Newsham Park allotments. The only damage was to empty stables in Sandforth Road.

On the 4th January, two alerts were given and aircraft were sighted on each occasion.

January 6th, 7th and 8th saw brief visits by single enemy aircraft which flew high over the city. Things really appeared to be slackening, and the city was preparing to give a guarded sigh of relief.

But at 7.37 p.m. on January 8th, a heavy bomber force of approximately 200 aircraft was reported to be heading for the Liverpool area. The raiders approached the city from all angles and at varying heights, in an endeavour to evade the intense anti-aircraft barrage. Many aircraft were reported damaged by our night-fighters based at Hooton and Woodvale and at least one aircraft was brought down in the sea near the Welsh coast.

High-explosive bombs were dropped on the South Docks and the Dingle Oil Depot, where serious damage was caused to warehouses and sheds at the South Herculaneum Dock.

During the raid, incendiary bombs were dropped over a wide area of the city. A number of houses were demolished in Virgil Street by high-explosive bombs, and fires broke out in the Everton district.

A Dutch barn was burned down at Holt's Farm, Gateacre, and the Police Station at Everton Terrace was slightly damaged when an incendiary bomb fell through the roof.

A vicarage was damaged and a high-explosive bomb demolished the stand at the White City Greyhound Track.

However, the casualties throughout the area were amazingly light, considering that this massive raid lasted six hours. On the 11th January, raiders were again reported in the vicinity of Merseyside, but no bombs were dropped.

Members of the Auxiliary Fire Service take a tea-break on the morning of 5th May 1941.

What remained of the Ernest Brown Technical School, Durning Road, Liverpool, after it was struck by a landmine. Many of the 300 who sheltered there were killed. This picture was not passed by the censor until the end of 1943.

There were many casualties when Mill Road Hospital was hit during the May blitz, but some 400 patients and staff were rescued.

Salvage work: Sidney Place, Edge Hill, Liverpool, 12th November 1940.

This was once their home ...

On the 13th January, raiders were driven back by a fierce anti-aircraft barrage.

The following night, 14th January, aircraft were reported over the area but again no incidents occurred.

During the month, 53 people were killed and 41 were seriously injured.

February 1941

Air raid sirens were sounded on the 1st, 5th, 10th and 12th February, when raiders made a brief visit to the area.

On the 5th, a single bomb was dropped on a row of houses, killing three people and at Stockport in Cheshire, two people were seriously injured when their house collapsed. Whether that raider was lost from an intended mission against Merseyside or Manchester will never be known.

On the 15th, three alerts were sounded. No incidents were reported during the first, but during the second raid, a large number of incendiary bombs were dropped on the Aigburth area. During the third raid of the night, many high-explosive and incendiary bombs were dropped on the North End of the city, and a Post Office garage in Commercial Road was demolished.

Casualties sustained during the month were 2 killed and 7 seriously injured.

March 1941

The beginning of March brought enemy reconnaissance aircraft over the city on the 5th, 7th, 10th and 11th. On the evening of the 12th came a heavy attack. The first incident took place at 7.14 p.m. and the second wave of bombers was reported at 8.29 p.m. Flares were dropped, followed by bombs and parachute mines. The main wave of the attack seemed to be centred on the docks and the Cheshire side of the river, where considerable damage was done to houses in Birkenhead and Wallasey.

In Birkenhead, the General Hospital had to be evacuated when the roof was set on fire. Many demands were made on the Fire Service during the right and, in one district, 150 people were evacuated from their homes.

In Liverpool 126 fires were dealt with by the Fire Brigade and the A.F.S. Serious fires were at the Head Post Office, Victoria Street (which has to this day a curious 'cut-off' look at the top where it lost its top storey and roof), and also at South John Street Telephone Exchange, the Cotton Exchange, and the Municipal Annexe in Dale Street.

Because of the intensity of the fires, Fire Brigades were brought into the area from other districts. During the raid, two sports grounds were damaged and a sanatorium received a direct hit, killing one person and injuring six.

On the 13th March there was a light attack, following what had been apparently a reconnaissance raid earlier the same evening. The raid lasted till 2.14 a.m. and many aircraft took part.

Birkenhead and Wallasey suffered extensive damage and serious fire damage was caused to private property.

In Liverpool, extensive damage was caused by a bomb at S.3 Alexandra Dock Shed and two ships were sunk in the river after striking mines.

'Chandelier' flares were dropped at a number of points but were shot out by tracer bullets before they became fully ignited.

One tragic incident occurred when a heavy-calibre bomb dropped in the middle of a blazing building, hurling firemen high into the air. It killed six and injured many others.

That night, at about the time the cinemas and theatres were closing, people had the excitement of watching a duel between a Night Fighter and a Heinkel 111 bomber. An eye-witness gave this account:

> "Just as I was leaving home to go on night duty, my attention was attracted by the sound of machine-gun fire, which I thought was directed towards flares which had just been dropped. Then I noticed the plumes of condensed air from the plane. Travelling along the plume could be seen tracer bullets from a fighter hot in pursuit. "He's after him, it's one of ours" I cried. My wife and neighbours came and joined me and we all shouted for joy when we saw, at the front of the smoke plume, a ball of fire. Suddenly there was a tremendous explosion and bits and pieces of debris started falling away from the aircraft as it plunged into a recreation ground three miles away."

The next evening varicoloured flares were dropped by bombers; at least 270 incendiary bombs fell on the Speke district, setting fire to houses and slightly damaging the aircraft factory that was situated there. Again, evidence of what must have been very worrying accuracy in finding vital targets—though the Germans were, of course, not worried how many civilians they killed in the process.

Nine high-explosive bombs were dropped near Kirkby Railway Station; four fell on railway-sidings and the others caused damage to the permanent way.

On the 15th March, the famous "Mammoth"—the Mersey Docks and Harbour Board's floating crane—was sunk by two bombs while lying in the West Float Dock, Birkenhead. She sank stern first, on an even keel; her great jib was undamaged and was later removed before she could be raised. It took 17 months, at a cost of £21,500 to restore her to service.

On the 16th March, a rescue party working at Lancaster Avenue, Wallasey, heard a faint cry from the debris of a house. Rescue workers tore away at the debris and found a small child, a few months old, lying half-buried amongst the rubble. The little girl had lain there since the 12th March and near her body lay both her parients, dead.

An Air Ministry statement, issued on the 18th March, indicated that on the nights of the 12th and 13th March alone, five hundred people were killed and five hundred were seriously injured. The official figures for the month were 578 killed and 632 injured.

April 1941

There were three main raids in this month. On the 7th April at 9.35 pm, night-fighters reported to their control that a large bomber force was heading towards Merseyside. It was later estimated by the Air Ministry that at least 75 enemy aircraft took part in the raid. At least two of these were brought down.

Many people in the North End of the city of Liverpool witnessed a dog-fight between a Heinkel 111 and a Defiant night fighter. They saw a small circle of light gradually grow into a mass of flames as the aircraft dived on to Bank Marsh in the Ribble Estuary. One crew member was found alive, but nearby lay the charred body of another airman. The remains of his parachute harness were still strapped to his body. Portions of another body were found nearby. A second plane was blown to pieces in the air when its bomb load exploded over the South End of the city.

At least 200 explosive incendiary-bombs were dropped in the neighbourhood of Beaconfield Road, and a further 50 of the same type were dropped on the Garston district. Two hundred were also reported in the Menlove Avenue area, and the Lister Drive Power Station suffered damage when an incendiary bomb struck the roof.

Twenty-six nuns had a remarkable escape when a high-explosive bomb wrecked a convent in the Edge Lane area and a large chapel adjacent to the convent was also damaged. But the altar-vases and candlesticks were unscathed despite the fact that the large window and many of the furnishings were severely damaged.

During the same raid, a high-explosive bomb struck a school, and an Auxiliary Fire Service post was slightly damaged. Although this raid lasted for over six hours, there were remarkably few casualties.

On the 14th April, an enemy raider flew over the city at a great height. Later in the evening, a small number of incendiary bombs was dropped. On the 15th April a raid lasting several hours took place, but again the damage was light. A golf course on the outskirts of the city was badly holed!

It would appear that the raid was a 'shadow attack' to divert the night fighters from the main bomber force which that night attacked Belfast for several hours, aiming for the shipyards there. Whole sections of the city were laid in ruins, and the failure in the water-supply left the fires unchecked. The Belfast A.R.P. and the Fire Services did their varied tasks courageously. From the less affected parts of the city, volunteers came in their hundreds. Fire-fighting reinforcements were even rushed across the Irish Sea from the mainland. More surprisingly, help came from Eire, which maintained an uneasy neutrality throughout the war (since many Irishmen felt—and some still feel—that any enemy of Britain was a friend of theirs). But the moment the need was realised, volunteer firemen from the neutral state came racing through the night—and with their peace-time headlamps full on!

When morning broke, parts of the city of Belfast were an awesome sight. The ruined fringe roads were blocked by heaps of smoking debris and acrid smelling craters. Water ran through the rubble, gas-mains spurted fountains of flames. It was estimated that at least 100 enemy aircraft were engaged in that attack.

Five days later, on the 21st April, a reconnaissance aircraft was spotted, but no bombs were dropped.

On 23rd and 24th April, further reconnaissance flights were carried out without incident; but on the 26th, a high-explosive bomb damaged a Babies Home.

During the month, 44 persons were killed and 125 were seriously injured.

May 1941

The month of May 1941 will live long in the memory of those who experienced and survived the now famous 'May Blitz', as it will forever be known. On May 1st, the attacks were comparatively light. There were fewer than one hundred incidents in Liverpool and none in Bootle, but casualties did occur in suburban areas of Birkenhead. During that night, it was thought that a large-scale onslaught was imminent, as large numbers of enemy aircraft were heading towards the area. However, the attack faded out. One raider was brought down and another plane blew up in the air over the city, its wreckage falling into the Mersey.

One bomb, however, did blast the front of a wholesale tobacconist's shop. In a public house opposite, a docker moaned "if it's not the bloody pubs they're after, it's the ciggies".

Another bomb demolished an emergency Rest Centre, killing twelve W.V.S. women who were preparing meals for the homeless.

The following night, May 2nd, the scale of the attack was doubled, with repeated relays of enemy planes crossing the city. The anti-aircraft barrage forced them to climb to a great height, with the result that their bombs were dropped at random.

The Anderson shelters, foreground left (named after the wartime Home Secretary Sir John Anderson) save many lives. Here there were no casualties in spite of the fact that the bomb dropped only five feet away.

Often the family pets were the sole survivors of bombed homes, and were cared for by neighbours.

Night-fighters shot down five bombers and one aircraft was brought down by flying into the steel cables suspended from barrage balloons. During the raid, thousands of incendiary bombs were dropped over a wide area. High-explosive bombs were then dropped into the middle of burning buildings—the normal procedure, as incendiaries were a dual-purpose weapon: to burn buildings and also thereby provide visual markers for further bombing.

Without doubt, the most sensational incident of that night was the blowing up of the Brocklebank Steamer *Malakand*, lying at the South West side of the Huskisson Dock No. 2.

The *Malakand* had 1,000 tons of ammunition in her holds, which was destined for the Middle East. For four hours, her captain, crew and fire-brigade fought heroically to save the ship and to prevent the fire from reaching the explosive cargo but, at approximately 4 am the first of many explosions occurred. Part of the ship's plates were thrown high in the air, some to a distance of two-and-a-half miles. One of her four-ton anchors was found over 100 yards away, on top of a sunken steam hopper. Whole dock-sheds disappeared along with the nearest Overhead Railway Station.

For seventy-four hours the ship continued to explode but, despite the damage that was done, only four people were killed. Two of them, a man and his wife, were motoring along the dock road when a steel plate sliced into their car. One dockboard employee was blown off his feet and, as he lay there, a large buckled ships plate fell across his body, covering him like an Anderson Shelter. Apart from being in a state of shock he was uninjured.

Here, with the kind permission of Captain H.C. Kinley through Mr. Tony Roper, is a letter which was sent by the ship's Master to the Fire Service authorities. It was, of course, top secret at the time.

> "Dear Sir,
>
> Amongst the general cargo the *Malakand* was carrying were 1,000 tons of high explosive bombs. These were stored in Nos. 1, 3 and 6 hatches and at approximately 11.15 pm on May 3rd, 1941, some short time after the air raid warning siren had sounded, and when there was a great deal of air activity going on, a partly inflated barrage balloon fell on the for'ard deck of my ship over the No. 1 hatch and started to blaze fiercely; pumps were got to work and within fifteen minutes the fire was put out by members of the crew. While the engagement with the burning balloon was taking place, a shower of incendiaries and several high explosive bombs fell on the neighbouring dock sheds; some incendiaries also fell on the deck of the *Malakand* but these were successfully dealt with.
>
> Around midnight, a shed on the East side was utterly demolished and the ruins raged fiercely. The shed on the South side was also violently ablaze and it appeared that the water

played on it for quenching purposes only intensified the flames when it contacted the goods stored inside. The whole shed soon became a raging inferno, and the flames from it spread to the *Malakand*, enveloping the ship from stem to stern. It soon became apparent that the flames were fast becoming too strong for our meagre fire appliances; the heat too was proving overpowering to the men, so I gave the order to abandon ship.

We left via the ship's gangway and made our way along the quayside to a point where the shed was least affected by fire.

Immediately I contacted the nearest Auxiliary Fire Station, which was situated at North West Huskisson No. 1 but found it unattended as all personnel were engaged in fire fighting at the adjacent dock sheds. I went over to them, found the officer in charge, John Lappin, and acquainted him with the state of the fire on board my ship, and also of the dangerous cargo she carried. Mr. Lappin immediately 'phoned from his station to his headquarters and asked for assistance, stating the facts as I had given them. After this, he employed all available hands of the *Malakand* to work on the fire alongside his own men, and his patience and tenacity as a leader aroused the admiration of all who witnessed it. He had little equipment, insufficient men and the scene of the fire was a continuous target for the enemy bombers which seemed to ceaselessly dive-bomb over us, yet he pursued his arduous task unflinchingly, and the men at his command with admirable courage carried out his instructions.

I realised the danger of the men, who, led by Mr. Lappin, continued their endeavour to penetrate the blazing wall of shed fires to reach the ship. Several times I put the dangerous situation to him, but although he and his men knew well the extent of their danger, they would not be deterred; Mr. Lappin replying that such risks were demanded of the fire service.

Around 3 am Mr. Lappin decided to go personally to acquaint the Chief Officer of the Fire Brigade with the facts of the situation and the urgency of the assistance it required by telephone. I accompanied him and, along with him, spoke to Chief Officer Owen, who agreed to send a special tender with Oxy-acetylene burning apparatus to enable us to cut a hole in the port-side of the ship, in the hope of scuttling her. We then returned to the scene of the fire and the promised tender had duly arrived. But the ship exploded before anyone could approach to sink her.

Several men were injured when the explosion took place, myself included, and I regret to have to state that lives were lost.

Yours faithfully,
(Sgd) H.C. Kinley

During the same night, five people were killed and many injured when a high-explosive bomb struck a church in a thickly-populated area. The bomb bounced off the roof and penetrated the side aisle, falling down into the hall below, where 350 people were sheltering. An eyewitness, Mr. T. O'Brien gave this account:

> "I was standing with some other people in the passage near the crypt, when we heard an explosion and the crash of glass from the church above us. Fortunately for us, the passage was reinforced, which helped to take most of the blast, but some of the masonry was dislodged and crashed down on the people."

A Mr. J. Gordon—an A.R.P. Warden— also narrowly escaped death when a bomb wrecked his Sector Post and a public-house nearby, trapping a woman and child.

Another bomb landed in a cemetery and four hospitals in the area had narrow escapes. Many fire-watchers saw a raider shot down by anti-aircraft fire. Large scale damage was caused to dock property and the tug *Hornby* was sunk at her moorings.

A Mr. L. Philbin said

> "I was holding my 18 month old son in my arms when, without any warning, the door was blown inwards and finished up on its side, six inches away from the baby. The strange thing is, he added, that it was the first time we had ever stayed up because of a raid. Something told my wife and I not to go to bed."

But for this chance, the Philbins might have been killed, as the blast smashed a large hole in the ceiling above their bed and heavy pieces of masonry demolished the bedroom.

May 3rd appeared to be the most heavy and determined attack by the Germans as they attempted to bring Liverpool and the rest of Merseyside to its knees. From early evening until dawn, wave upon wave of heavy bombers swept the area, raining high-explosive, incendiary bombs and parachute mines over a wide area. Large fires ranged from the North End of the docks to the Dingle in the South. Hundreds were killed and injured, as fire-fighters strove to quell the flames. Business premises, hospitals, tenements and private houses were all indiscriminately bombed.

Mossley Hill Hospital received a direct hit from a high-explosive bomb. The same hospital had the misfortune to be one of the early victims of the raid, and the whole of the rescue work was carried out to the accompaniment of falling bombs, gunfire and conflagration.

It is a measure of the heroism of all concerned that, during the height of what the Germans claimed to be one of the heaviest raids ever launched against this country, some 400 patients from the hospital were rescued from the shattered buildings and assembled, then driven through the shell-spattered streets to other institutions and that the whole of the work was completed four hours after the hit was sustained.

In view of the extent of the damage inflicted upon the hospital, several wards, the X-ray and emergency departments and the ambulance station were completely wrecked. It is remarkable that casualties were not heavier; here, for the first time, is the account of what happened inside the hospital after it was hit:

> After the first explosion, fire broke out in the Ambulance and Mobile First Aid Posts, causing serious damage. At the time of the incident, an operation was being performed upon a young Greek seaman named Dutches. He was an emergency case, requiring an immediate abdominal operation; he was prepared and actually in the hands of the surgeon, who had made the first incision, when the heavy bomb exploded in the Maternity Ward above the Operating Theatre bringing down walls, floors and heavy blocks of masonry.
>
> The surgeon was killed outright, a sister on the other side of the table was buried, and her body was not recovered until three days later. Others in the Theatre were also killed, whilst the patient lay in a cloud of dust untouched and was found later by hospital porters who climbed through the piles of rubble to him.
>
> In the light of torches, it was quickly ascertained that the man had still a chance, although by this time, his condition was critical. Nurses and doctors quickly took measures to staunch the incisions and prepare him for the three-mile dash in an ambulance to another hospital, where Dutches safely arrived and was immediately rushed to the Operating Theatre.
>
> He later recovered, not knowing of his ordeal, having already been anaesthetized for his operation. Seventeen members of the staff, fifteen ambulance drivers and thirty patients were killed, with a further seventy seriously injured."

During the same raid, in the early hours of the morning, severe damage was caused to cultural and other famous buildings in Liverpool. The Museum, the Technical College, the Rotunda Theatre and Lewis's Stores were but a few of the places hit.

Extensive damage was done to Liverpool Public Library in William Brown Street. Some parts of the Library escaped but nothing remained of the old and original portion which was built in 1860, the gift to the City from Sir William Brown. The Museum and Public Library both lost precious and irreplaceable exhibits and historic material.

The Administrative and the Catalogue Departments of the Library were completely destroyed, and The Board Room and The Music Library were gutted. The small Lecture Room, in which the Liverpool Parliamentary

The much loved Argyle Theatre, Birkenhead, where some of the greatest stars of the British theatre and music-hall played.

Devastation at the top of Bold Street, Liverpool, after the night of 5/6th May 1941.

Rescuers searching the wreckage of a home in Huntley Road, Sheil Road, Liverpool, 16th September 1940.

Debating Society had held its meetings for many years, was completely destroyed by fire. But in the strong room below ground level, many valuable documents—including the Roscoe Letters, Gregson Papers and Herdman drawings of Old Liverpool—were saved.

The official estimate of the book losses in the badly damaged part of the building, was 150,000 volumes valued at £112,000. These did not include the large collection of Parliamentary Papers, in itself a serious loss.

Fortunately, the Picton Reading Room and its collection of books escaped with minor damage, as did also the Hornby Art Library and the Picton Lecture Hall.

Of the public museums adjoining the Central Library, all that was left standing was the Administrative Block and the Shipping and British Zoology Galleries, both slightly damaged by water.

In the basement, the Aquarium, containing a seal as well as many fish was destroyed, and the livestock perished.

The Rotunda Theatre was completely burnt out. It held the distinction of being the only Liverpool Theatre marked as a stopping-place on tram tickets. It was a well-known landmark in the Scotland Road area and was familiarly known as 'The Old Roundy'; built as a music hall more than 80 years ago, the Rotunda had been burnt down in 1866. And of course, long after it vanished, the name survives as familiarly as if it had never been destroyed.

The Bluecoat Chambers, formally the Liverpool Blue Coat Hospital (which was saved from demolition in 1929) was severely damaged by fire. All that remained after the raid was the west wing, housing the Sandon Studios and a large meeting room on the ground floor of the central portion. The large concert hall above was gutted, leaving only the stage and part of the proscenium.

Liverpool's Little Theatre at the premises of the Playgoers' Club, housed in the east wing, was completely destroyed.

The administrative work of the Liverpool Diocese was greatly hampered when their building, Church House in South John Street, was completely wrecked. The premises of the Liverpool Law Society which was situated in Cook Street, Castle Street and Harrington Street, the largest institution of its kind outside London, were gutted completely, and an extensive Law Library of some 350,000 law volumes was destroyed.

Liverpool Cathedral, on the same night, had a remarkable escape from serious damage when a high-explosive bomb struck the south east transept. The bomb pierced the roof, striking the top of the inner brick wall that supports the transept's central beam, and was deflected outwards. It then crashed through the outer wall and exploded in the air over the street. Had it by chance been deflected inwards, it would have gone through the ceiling, several feet below the roof and would have caused havoc within the cathedral itself.

A great number of stained-glass windows were damaged to some extent by blast and bomb splinters. The Derby Memorial transept window—a particularly large stained-glass window was completely blown out. The Golden Window and the Sapphire Window were slightly damaged, and every window in the Lady Chapel was damaged to some extent.

A large fire broke out when incendiary-bombs fell into the contractor's yard at the west end of the cathedral, where offices, a setting-out shed and sawing-machinery used for cutting the stone were situated. Damage was done, but fortunately the prevailing wind carried the flames across St. James's Road and away from the great building.

An old Liverpool church, St. Luke's, Bold Street, was gutted by fire; only the burnt out shell remains today, though lovingly restored as a memorial to the courage and fortitude of the people of Liverpool during the blitz. Very few of the church contents were saved except the lectern, two memorial chairs, a memorial desk and part of the altar cross. The bells of St. Luke's crashed to the ground soon after the fire had obtained a fierce hold, and every one of the stained-glass windows was destroyed.

In the same raid, St. Michael's Church (Pitt Street) was also razed to the ground.

A most striking example of heroism occurred when a bomb hit an ammunition train at Clubmoor, setting it on fire. As waggon after waggon blew up, railwaymen with complete indifference to danger uncoupled the rear section of the train and shunted it away.

Mr. Norman Tunna, a shunter, who climbed into a railway truck where incendiary bombs were blazing on top of a load of mines, was the first Merseyside man to win the George Cross. Mr. Tunna related his experience in these words:

> "I ran to the engine at the head of the train and got a bucket of water to throw on the burning waggon. Then I secured a stirrup-pump. By this time, two other men had arrived and we sprayed water on the waggon and eventually put the fire out. I then saw another truck on fire and climbed onto it, and, lifting aside the tarpaulin sheets, saw two ignited incendiary bombs blazing away between a load of 250 lb high-explosive bombs. I made a grab at one of the incendiaries and tried to retrieve it but it was wedged between two of the bombs. A driver brought me a shunting pole and I was able to force the bombs apart. I then reached down for the incendiary and threw it out of harm's way. By this time the bombs in the waggon had got very hot with the heat from the burning incendiaries, so I decided to spray them with water. Fortunately, none of the bombs exploded."

During the same raid, Mr. P.J. Mahoney won the George Medal for leading his gang into fighting the fire and discharging cases of explosive fuses onto

Ballantyne Road, West Derby, Liverpool, where many people were killed by a landmine during the night raid of 26th April 1941.

"How many were in there?" A hurried conference of rescue workers in Ranleigh Road, Edge Lane, Liverpool.

Firemen, ARP wardens and civilians searching for survivors in Virgil Street, Liverpool, after the night raid of 9/10th January 1941.

the railway. Another George Medal and an O.B.E. were also awarded on that occasion.

Linacre Gas Works, situted near the dock estate, was attacked and sustained serious damage during a raid on May 3rd/4th. High-explosive bombs fell on No. 5 and No. 8 holders exploding internally. The resulting blast tore off the down-sheeting and set the escaping gas on fire. No. 8 holder was later repaired with the whole of the inner lift being re-built and re-sheeted.

Holders No. 1, 2, 3, 4 and 7 were also seriously damaged by blast, shrapnel and falling debris. No. 3 holder was riddled with splinters and escaping gas set on fire. The holders required some 500 patches before going back into service.

The first high-explosive bomb to fall on the Works dropped just after midnight, followed by a second bomb which landed in the same crater. These two bombs fractured a 42 inch diameter water/gas main and a 30 inch coal/gas main and, at the same time, completely destroyed the fitting shop at the De-tarrer House.

The De-tarrer connecting mains were fractured and the vessels were torn from their foundations and were found peppered with shrapnel holes and leaning at 45 degrees against the Exhauster House wall.

The same night, bombs also fell at the side of the C.W.G. Purifying House, seriously damaging the building and breaking off the gas mains supply to the plant.

On the following Thursday, 7th May, a parachute-mine fell on the experimental works and completely demolished it. The resulting blast and flying debris caused extensive damage to the surrounding buildings.

Later in the year, the same gas works suffered considerable damage when a high-explosive bomb completely destroyed No. 6 holder, releasing one-and-a-half million cubic feet of gas, which exploded. In addition, No. 2 and No. 4 holders and other property were damaged by incendiary bombs.

On May 4th, 5th and 6th, attacks were moderately light. On the 7th, severe damage was caused in the two boroughs with over three hundred incidents being reported. Extensive and serious fires raged in the docks and much damage was caused to private property at New Brighton in the early hours of May 7th. The ferryboat *Royal Daffodil* II was sunk at her moorings at Seacombe Landing Stage.

On May 8th, the area received seven scattered raids from 10.45 pm to 4.00 am and, during this time relays of bombers crossed the city, showering it with incendiary bombs. Casualties were light, despite an underground shelter receiving a direct hit.

At Wallasey, extensive damage was caused to house property, which entailed the evacuation of 7,500 people.

On the 15th, 22nd and 25th May, sirens were sounded in the area but no incidents were reported. On May 28th, three Heinkel 111 bombers were driven off after dropping their bombs at random over two heavily-populated areas. Rescue workers digging at one house heard a voice calling from beneath the rubble, "Hello there! Hello there, wack! Get me out!" After a quarter of an hour and much effort they reached—a parrot. When the cage was uncovered, the parrot blinked up at his rescuers and said "Hello, Hello! I thank you, I thank you!". Or so the story went at the time, probably after much retelling over many a pint of Higson's.

The following night, 29th, one incident was reported when a single bomb killed a man standing at his front door. On the night of the 30th May, the enemy sent a heavy bomber-force against Liverpool, but the raid was diverted due to a fierce anti-aircraft fire and fighter protection. A Beaufighter claimed a Dornier. An eyewitness described it as "a small ball of orange fire, which grew in size for a few seconds, then trailed away meteor-like in a mass of brilliant sparks".

Flares were dropped over the Dingle and Aigburth areas but were immediately shot out by flaming 'onions' and tracer bullets.

On the Pier Head, damage was caused to the Liver Buildings and the Mersey Docks and Harbour Board offices, the latter being severely damaged internally by fire. High-explosive bombs also destroyed the Corn Exchange in Fenwick Street.

So ended the most extraordinary episode in the history of the city. Statistics show that Liverpool, Birmingham and Plymouth were top of the table, with eight major raids each over the blitz period, followed by Bristol with six.

'May Week' will never be forgotten by Liverpudlians. It indicated the savagery of the raiders who wreaked havoc on Liverpool and the neighbouring boroughs of Bootle, Birkenhead and Wallasey. Houses, shops and rest centres were badly damaged or destroyed. In Bootle, all but one of the rest centres were put out of action. It was therefore not surprising that much shifting of the population took place. Maghull, Formby and Ormskirk became refugee areas. In Maghull, during the course of one evening, 6,000 people were accommodated throughout the town in church and school halls and in private residences. 'Chinatown', formerly closer to the docks, was re-established in the Great George Square area, where it took root and remains to this day.

Despite inconvenience and suffering, morale in general was high but lurid rumours flourished. The I.R.A. and Fifth Columnists continued with their campaign of spreading fear and rumour, but the police and Civil Defence services were well aware of it. For example, Civil Defence Report No. 22, covering the period 1st September 1940 to the 29th September 1940, told the War Cabinet that morale in Liverpool continued to be good but admitted that the police was seriously concerned about friction between indigenous inhabitants and unofficial evacuees from the bombed areas in the south. One full-time mass observer latched on to some of the undertones of the frictions

Buchanan's Flour Mills, Birkenhead, devastated in the March blitz 1941.

Pollard's Garage (now Cubbin & North), Ullet Road, on 5th September 1940. All the buried cars were recovered in working order, only slightly dented. They were made of stronger metal in those days!

The centre of Birkenhead after the night raid of 1st October 1940.

secretly reported on May 17th:

> "General Morale: Very Unsteady. This has been a week of gruesome rumours:
>
> (a) Trainloads of unidentified corpses have been sent from Merseyside for mass burial or cremation.
>
> (b) Homeless and hungry people are marching around bombed areas carrying white flags and howling protests.
>
> (c) Food riots are taking place.
>
> (d) Martial law is being considered.
>
> (e) Letters are being censored in and out of the City."

None of this, of course, was anywhere near the truth. Casualties figures were grossly exaggerated, and rumours circulated that over 20,000 women and children had been killed during the week. Many of the most responsible Liverpool citizens believed that a demonstration for peace had been staged and the story was still current years later. There was no such demonstration, or anything remotely like it.

But despite the rumours, casualties were high. In Liverpool alone 1,453 persons were killed and 1,065 seriously injured. In Bootle, 257 men, women and children were killed and 26 seriously injured; and 5 persons were unaccounted for. In Birkenhead, 28 people were killed and 44 seriously injured; and in Wallasey 3 were killed and 19 seriously injured. The total casualty figures for the four boroughs during May were 1,741 killed and 1,154 seriously injured. Countless numbers of cherished domestic pets also perished: not a matter likely to influence the final outcome of any war, but nevertheless a potential blow to the morale of those closely affected.

June, 1941

June 1st saw a brief attack by five enemy aircraft; no bombs were dropped.

On the 21st June, night fighters successfully drove off six Heinkel 111 bombers as they approached the River Mersey.

On the 24th, a small bomber force succeeded in penetrating the area, and on the 25th June a sharp attack was made which ended in the destruction of 2 enemy aircraft over the sea.

Three persons were killed during this month on Merseyside.

July, 1941

July 6th and 24th saw two brief attacks in which two surface shelters were destroyed, killing and injuring the occupants. A number of bombs fell on the foreshore at Dingle, injuring no-one except a number of fish which were found high and dry on the mud.

August, 1941

There were no incidents during this month except that raiders were seen on numerous occasions heading towards the north-west but were driven off.

September, 1941

September 27th, in the late evening, a single bomber dropped a bomb killing a fire-watcher on duty.

October, 1941

On October 12th, a single plane attacked the area. The raid lasted one hour. Little damage was caused and it was believed that this aircraft was brought down over the sea.

On October 20th, the Germans made what appeared at first to be a determined attack on the port, but were met by five Beaufighters which successfully turned them away from the city, bringing one aircraft down. However, one aircraft evaded the fighters and swooped, with engines turned off, on to a housing estate causing numerous casualties.

Two nights later, 22nd October, three bombers were shot down by the Liverpool defences. One was brought down in flames, killing two of its crew. The remaining three who bailed out were captured by the Home Guard. One bomb fell on a brewery storage shed, killing a man and severely injuring another.

On the night of the 26th October, an air raid warden was killed when two heavy bombs destroyed some cottages.

November, 1941

After an interval of nearly a week, the enemy made what appeared to be its final visit to the area, causing casualties and two fatalities on the 2nd November. One bomber was destroyed.

The following day people looked at its smoking wreckage which had killed its three occupants. Parts of the machine—a Junkers 88—lay strewn about in a field. Pieces of parachute were also picked up but the occupants had had time to bale out.

During the month it was disclosed by the Air Ministry that German bombers operating against Merseyside were carrying a fender or girder fixed in the nose of the machine as a defence against the Balloon Barrage.

It was estimated that the fenders weighed 600 to 800 lbs, which slowed down the bomber and reduced the bomb and petrol load. It was also believed that it was almost impossible to fly the aircraft on one engine as the fender reduced the speed by 19 mph and would thus cause quicker stalling. It should be remembered that, compared to the modern jet, aircraft of World War II flew very slowly indeed.

It remains to record briefly the visits of some of the distinguished people who visited the City of Liverpool, Merseyside and the port and defence installations that played such a vital part in eventually bringing the war to a victorious conclusion.

Beteen May and December 1940, and October 1941 and November 1942, King George VI came repeatedly to Merseyside to see the extent of the damage. On the first and fourth visits he was accompanied by Queen Elizabeth. His personal distress and feelings of grief were plainly visible as he walked among his people, and on more than one occasion it was reported that while giving sympathetic handshakes he quietly left a £1 note behind (a not inconsiderable sum in those days).

In September 1940, the late Duke of Kent visited the Port and on various dates between 1942-1944 King Haakon of Norway, the Maharajah of Kashmir and Queen Juliana (then Princess) of the Netherlands visited the area. Mr. and Mrs. Churchill were twice in the city in 1941, followed by Mr. Attlee, Lord Woolton (who had, of course, been an executive at Lewis's store) and Mrs. Roosevelt, the wife of the U.S. President.

Among the most memorable of the many visitors was the world famous singer, the late Count John McCormack who, with the band of the Irish Guards, sang in the rain to the dockers at the Gladstone Dock.

Such, then, was 'The Liverpool Blitz of 1940-1941'. Winston Churchill wrote:

> "I see the damage done by the enemy attacks, but I also see, side-by-side with the devastation, and amid the ruins, quiet, confident, bright and smiling eyes, beaming with consciousness of being associated with a cause far higher and wider than any of human or personal issue. I see the spirit of an unconquered people".

Some Facts and Figures
concerning the Merseyside Blitz
and released only after the war

- Considerably more than half the houses in the four boroughs were damaged, and 10,000 completely destroyed. Bootle had the amazing proportion of 16,000 of its 17,000 houses damaged.

  Liverpool's losses were (the figures in brackets indicate the number of houses in 1939):-

Liverpool:	(202,000)	destroyed 5,598,	damaged 124,989
Bootle:	(17,189)	destroyed 2,013,	damaged 16,300
Birkenhead:	(35,727)	destroyed 2,079,	damaged 26,000
Wallasey:	(27,600)	destroyed 1,150,	damaged 17,000

- During the May raids 51,000 homeless people were cared for in Liverpool and another 25,000 in Bootle. During the whole raid period about 200,000 people passed through the rest centres after having to leave their homes.

- Through the whole period the P.A.C. served 250,000 meals from Mobile Canteens. During the May blitz they served for street feeding:-

  25,000 gallons of tea
  2,000 gallons of Scouse (i.e. Irish stew)
  21,000 Dinners
  360,000 Sandwiches

- At one time 9,000 workers from outside and 2,680 troops were assisting the City's own full resources of man power in May 1941, to open up the streets and remove the dangerous debris.

- Eighteen firemen were killed and 180 injured in May, when fighting the hundreds of fires which burned for days. Firemen from thirty-nine boroughs were brought in to help those already here and 550 fire-fighting appliances were added from outside.

- On May 14th, 1941, a mass funeral was held at Anfield Cemetery at which 1,000 victims of the May raids were buried in a common grave.

- To defend Liverpool's buildngs, 8,000,000 sandbags were filled with 150,000 tons of sand brought from Formby shore.

- Liverpool's rescue parties, trained in the City's pioneer training centre (opened 1937) got out alive from under debris, 1,653 persons who had been buried from three to forty-eight hours.

- It cost £500,000 merely to clean up the City after the May blitz.

- On September 21st, 1940, at Anfield Park, Liverpool, British Welter-Weight Champion Ernie Roderick fought British Light-Weight Champion Eric Boon. An air raid was on at the time but the fight went the full distance and, despite the fact that anti-aircraft guns were firing and planes were seen over the ground, none of the 5,000 spectators left their seats.

- On May 8th, just after 10 pm, the beloved *Royal Daffodil* II was sunk at her moorings alongside Seacombe Landing Stage. She was a comparatively new ship, built at Cammell Laird's in 1934.

  Although only 150 ft. overall, she had the beam of a small liner and was powered by two 1,200 HP engines which gave her a speed of 12 knots—passenger capacity on ferry work was just under 2,000.

  From early days in the war, she, along with her sister ship, ferried American and Commonwealth troops and stood by the troopships if they were in trouble during air raids—ready to evacuate personnel at a moment's notice. A member of her crew gave this graphic account:-

  > "It was just past 10 pm on the 8th of May. The ship was 'Blacked-Out' and all 12 of us were below as shrapnel was raining down from exploding anti-aircraft shells. Suddenly there was a WHOOSH and a loud bang—and water came pouring in through a 60 foot hole near the starboard engine.
  >
  > My mate was on the engine room companion ladder at the time; next thing, he was blown out of the engine room and landed on the deck unhurt—except for his false teeth, they had gone!"

  How the *Royal Daffodil* II was sunk has never been satisfactorily explained—there are two theories:-

  (i) that the bomb exploded on impact, or
  (ii) went through the ship and exploded in the mud under it.

  Thirteen months passed before she surfaced again—her funnel and masts had gone—and she was covered in marine growth and full of silt and mud. Her starboard engine was smashed beyond repair but, by June 1943, she was back in service.

  After the war she was well-known as a River Dance and Cruise Ship. In the late fifties she was re-named the *St. Hilary*, her name being transferred to a new ship.

- On the morning of the 3rd May, metal foil strips measuring ten inches in length were found littered extensively throughout the area. The strips were dropped in large quantities from aircraft; their purpose was to disrupt the City's radar defences by jamming the wavelength and giving mis-coding echoes. The German code name was 'DÜPPEL'.

The Toll

Liverpool

	Killed	Seriously Injured
August, 1940	37	73
September, 1940	221	357
October, 1940	106	90
November, 1940	305	192
December, 1940	412	382
January, 1941	43	23
February, 1941	2	7
March, 1941	101	99
April, 1941	36	105
May, 1941	1,453	1,065

Bootle

	Killed	Seriously Injured
August, 1940	-	-
September, 1940	28	60
October, 1940	10	18
November, 1940	6	4
December, 1940	108	93
January, 1941	-	-
February, 1941	-	-
March, 1941	-	-
April, 1941	-	-
May, 1941	257	26
(plus missing)	5	

Birkenhead

	Killed	Seriously Injured
August, 1940	4	23
September, 1940	24	65
October, 1940	17	56
November, 1940	2	3
December, 1940	63	105
January, 1941	8	15
February, 1941	-	-

	Killed	Seriously Injured
March, 1941	288	275
April, 1941	8	20
May, 1941	28	44

Wallasey

	Killed	Seriously Injured
August, 1940	9	10
September, 1940	4	2
October, 1940	3	3
November, 1940	3	3
December, 1940	119	91
January, 1941	2	3
February, 1941	-	-
March, 1941	189	158
April, 1941	-	-
May, 1941	3	19

A Note on Sources

Most of the material in this book has been drawn from eye-witness accounts or personal experiences.

Government Papers

'An Investigation on Probable Air Raid Damage' dated June 1940. Reference HO/195/7X/L02120.

Military Training Pamphlets No. 45 of 13th April, 1942, Amendment No. 1 of 31st July, 1942 and June, 1943.

Newspapers and Periodicals

The Liverpool Echo.
Liverpool Daily Post.

Books

Harris, Air Chief Marshall Sir Arthur, *Bomber Offensive.* Collins, 1947.
Merchantmen at War. H.M.S.O., 1944.
Pile, General Sir Frederick, *Ack-Ack.* Harrap, 1949.
Roof Over Britain, The Official Story f the A.A. Defences, 1939-1942. H.M.S.O., 1943.
Bombers over Merseyside. Liverpool Daily Post and Echo, 1943.
An Everyday History of Liverpool and Merseyside, Vol.II. Scouse Press Reprint.

Acknowledgements

I would like to extend my gratitude to the following for providing information for this book:

Mr. Tony Roper; Captain H.C. Kinley, Captain of the s.s. *Malakand*; Mr. H. Winstanley, Chief Constable, Liverpool City Police; The Air Ministry and Admiralty; Picton Reference Library; Controller of H.M. Stationery Office for permission to take extracts from their publication *Front Line* and the War Office for permission to extract information from Military Training Pamphlet No. 45, 1942, Amendments No. 1 and No. 2. Rear Admiral E.N. Poland, C.B., C.B.E.; The Mersey Docks and Harbour Board for permission to quote from their booklet *Port at War* and also *The Liverpolitan* for permission to use material from their booklet *Merseyside Militant*; Phoebus Publishing Company for permission to copy drawings from *Special Editions of Bombers* 1939-1945.

Of the many friends who have contributed material and information, I would in particular like to express my thanks to Miss Smith, Archivist, and Mrs. Audrey Edwards, both of Picton Reference Library. The late Miss Saxon of the Library also assisted with research. Mrs. Jean Kerr provided patient help with editing, and expertly typed the manuscript.